OUR CONSTITUTION
THE MYTH THAT BINDS US

OUR CONSTITUTION
The Myth That Binds Us

ERIC BLACK

WESTVIEW PRESS
Boulder and London

Published in 1988 in the United States of America by Westview Press, Inc.; Frederick A. Praeger, Publisher; 5500 Central Avenue, Boulder, Colorado 80301.

Library of Congress Cataloging-in-Publication Data
Black, Eric.
  Our Constitution: the myth that binds us/by Eric Black.
    p. cm.
  ISBN 0-8133-0694-9. ISBN 0-8133-0695-7 (pbk.)
  1. United States—Constitutional history—Popular works.
2. United States. Constitutional Convention (1787) I. Title.
KF4541.Z9B49 1988
342.73′029—dc19
[347.30229]
                                                                87-30259
                                                                CIP

Printed and bound in the United States of America.

The paper used in this publication meets the requirements of the American National Standard for Permanence of Paper for Printed Library Materials Z39.48-1984.

10 9 8 7 6 5 4 3 2

To my parents,
Irving and Gladys Black

Acknowledgments

I gratefully acknowledge the guidance and general calming influence of Roger Buoen, who edited the series of articles on which this book is based. For reading drafts, discussing ideas and offering encouragement I am indebted to Tom and Ellie Hamburger, Cliff and Kim Greene, Mike and Barb Trangle, Paul Murphy, Daniel Farber, Suzannah Sherry and Dale Prentiss. And to Holly Johnson for all the above and more than I can say. Charlie Olson designed the pages and set the type. I thank John Ullmann for the title "The Myth that Binds Us" and the *Star Tribune* management for giving me my head instead of handing it to me.

Minneapolis, Minnesota   E.B.

Contents

Part Three:
Left Out of the Constitution

Part Four:
The Constitution in Our Times

Introduction

"The Founding Fathers."

The mere mention of the phrase conjures up glorious images of heroic Washington crossing the Delaware, shy-but-brilliant Jefferson writing "all men are created equal," fiery Patrick Henry demanding liberty or death and friendly old Ben Franklin stealing time from kite-flying to issue witty maxims.

"The Framers of the Constitution."

Those words cast the same men into clearer focus. There they stand, quill pens at the ready, gathered around a table in Philadelphia, creating the timeless document that would guide America from a loose collection of rebellious colonies to a pre-eminent superpower and a worldwide symbol of freedom, equality and democracy.

The picture is glorious and familiar. It reassures us about our country's past and its special place in the world. But, if we are interested in historical accuracy, we may have to make some changes. For example:

Airbrush Thomas Jefferson out of the "Framers" picture in your head. Although in a 1986 poll, Jefferson was the person most often identified as the primary author of our Constitution, he was in France at the time and had mixed feelings about the Constitutional Convention.

Patrick Henry wasn't in Philly either, but he didn't have mixed feelings about the project. He was unalterably opposed to holding the convention. Chosen to be a delegate, Henry refused to go, declaring he "smelt a rat." He hated the document produced in Philadelphia and hurled his considerable oratorical and political power against its ratification. He thought it was an aristocratic, anti-democratic charter, a grave threat to the sovereignty of the Commonwealth of Virginia and "the most fatal plan that could possibly be conceived to enslave a free people."

Former Chief Justice Warren Burger, chairman of the commission established to celebrate the bicentennial of the Constitution, called for the nation to use the bicentennial to give itself a "great civics and history lesson" on the meaning and origin of the

Constitution.

During the bicentennial year, the Star Tribune, Newspaper of the Twin Cities, assigned me to take Burger at his word.

I rummaged around in history books, law books and in the Constitution itself, looking at how it came to be written, how it has changed in two centuries and how it functions as "the Law of the Land."

In February of 1987, the newspaper's readers embarked with me on a series of Monday morning constitutionals. On 30 Mondays that year, the newspaper published the articles that form the basis of this book.

The theme that emerged in the articles is summarized in the title of this book. Our Constitution is the myth that binds us.

The Constitution is a document, sure enough, written 200 years ago and amended 26 times since. The whole thing fits on about 20 pages in a pocket-sized paperback. But the Constitution is much more than those few words on those few pages.

The much more is what I call the mythic Constitution.

The document and the myth together symbolize many things Americans believe in: democracy and liberty; legal equality of individuals and a balance of power among the branches of government; a nation of laws, not of men; majority rule and minority rights; one man, one vote; a free marketplace and the rights to free speech and privacy.

Some of these things were not mentioned in the original Constitution but have been added by amendment; yet in the mythic Constitution they have been extended back to the beginning of the Republic. Some are not mentioned in the document but have the power of law over us because we believe they are constitutional. Some are mentioned but not defined; their definition exists in the mythic Constitution, which includes 200 years of U.S. Supreme Court interpretations.

The power of the Supreme Court is an example of the mythic Constitution. The court's authority to rule on the constitutionality of acts of Congress makes it one of the three co-equal branches of the federal government.

Not only does the documentary Constitution never mention that the three branches should be co-equal, it never mentions the judicial power to strike down unconstitutional federal laws.

The court used the power only once in the first 70 years of Constitutional history and it was then a very dicey question whether the other two branches would let the court get away with it.

The second time the court used the power to strike down a federal law was one of the major disasters in constitutional history — the infamous Dred Scott decision of 1857 in which the court legalized slavery in the territories and greased the slope toward the Civil War. But even though the decision was much reviled, by 1857 the court's power to strike down a law had become part of the mythic Constitution and was beyond serious challenge, as it remains today.

Speaking of the Civil War, where does the documentary Constitution say states can't change their minds about being in the Union? It doesn't. The framers apparently never considered the question. But President Lincoln found such a principle in the mythic Constitution, and 120 years later most Americans probably would agree it's in there.

Thomas Jefferson once said that every generation should write its own constitution. The remark is sometimes used to suggest Jefferson was a poor prognosticator. After all, the charter written in his generation is still standing. But Jefferson's comment can be taken the opposite way, because every generation of Americans has indeed rewritten the Constitution to bring it into sync with contemporary values.

For example, the "equal protection" clause was written into documentary Constitution as part of the 14th Amendment in 1868. But it wasn't until 1954 that this language was interpreted to make it unconstitutional to overtly and explicitly segregate public schools. Not until 1971 did "equal protection" for the first time require a degree of legal equality for women.

Despite the evidence that our Constitution is always changing, we tend to extend its best qualities all the way back to the founding. This creates quite a strain between the facts of 1787 and our need to believe that the framers had their eyes on democracy, freedom, and equality.

The Constitution did not replace English royal tyranny with a new democracy. By 1787, when the framers did their framing, America had had a democracy for six years under the Articles of Confederation. The Constitution did not increase the democratic content of the system.

In fact, the deliberations began with the widely shared assumption that the chief defect of the 13 state constitutions was too much democracy. As Virginia Gov. Edmund Randolph said on the opening day of the convention: "None of the (state) constitutions have provided sufficient checks against democracy."

Under the new constitutional system, only one of the four power centers — the House of Representatives — would be elected by the people. Senators would be appointed by the state legislatures, as they were until this century. Supreme Court justices would be appointed by the president. And the Constitution did not require that the president be chosen by election. In fact, when Washington was elected two years later, only five states held popular votes.

As far as freedom and equality are concerned, the Constitution sanctioned the continuation of slavery and did nothing for women, Indians, minors or those who owned no property.

If you did own substantial property (as the framers did), the Constitution paid considerable attention to your rights — at least those rights relating to property.

But the rest of the rights we associate with the Constitution — freedom of religion, speech and press, the right to a fair trial and so on — were not included in the 1787 document. The framers decided against a Bill of Rights by a vote of 10 states to none. (Two state delegations had already left Philadelphia by the time that vote was taken and Rhode Island had never sent delegates.)

After a number of key states asked for a guarantee of rights during the ratification debates, James Madison promised to steer them through the first Congress. Madison, the leading theoretician at the Philadelphia convention and the man whom historians call "the father of the Constitution," considered the rights amendments unnecessary. But, true to his word, he fathered the Bill of Rights as well, while privately describing the task as a "nauseous project."

Even with the prospect of a Bill of Rights, ratification was only narrowly obtained in several states — and with no small amount of chicanery and political horse-trading.

Many of our deeply held beliefs about the framers are more myth than history. Yet it is our belief in those myths that gives our Constitution the power to bind us and to bind even the most powerful among us.

Ask yourself this.

Why did President Richard Nixon hand over the Watergate tapes containing evidence he must have known would end his presidency?

The first thing Nixon did when the tapes were subpoenaed was seek refuge in the mythic Constitution. He invoked "executive privilege," a concept not mentioned in the document. The Supreme Court didn't buy the argument and ruled he had to hand over the tapes.

So what? Nixon was the commander-in-chief of the greatest military power on the planet. The FBI, the CIA and the National Security Administration worked for him. The Supreme Court employed a few bailiffs, a few clerks, a few janitors.

Would Ferdinand Marcos, when he was president of the Philippines, have complied with an order from the Filipino Supreme Court to hand over evidence that would force him from office? After all, the Philippines had a constitution based on ours.

Marcos wouldn't have. But Nixon presided over a population that *believes* the Constitution gives the Supreme Court the power to order the president to comply with a congressional subpoena and *believes* everyone — even a president who carried 49 states in an election two years earlier — must submit to the Constitution.

We believe in the Constitution. There is an enormous nationwide consensus that the Constitution is supreme and can answer our most troubling national questions. That gives it the power to bind us.

Part One:
THE FOUNDING

1

Shays' Rebellion or Why the Framers Framed

Two hundred years ago, ragtag bands of American farmers bore arms against tyranny.

No, not the rebellion of the colonists against the British crown — Lexington and Concord, Valley Forge and all. That one ended in 1783 and, as you probably heard, the colonists won.

The insurrection that erupted in 1786-87 was Shays' Rebellion, named for Daniel Shays, one of its leaders. The rebels, many of them veterans of the War for Independence, were Western Massachusetts farmers who, like many farmers today, were drowning in debt and taxes.

They blamed their problems on the domination of the state by rich Boston merchants. The merchants, in return, blamed the farmers' complaints on laziness and greed.

When they failed to get relief from the Legislature or the courts, the farmers took up arms.

The brief and not-too-bloody rebellion sparked a humongous reaction among the ruling class. Just how humongous? How about this: The president of the U.S. Congress, the highest elected official in the country under the Confederation system, declared democracy to have been a failure and started shopping around Europe for a king to run the country.

We didn't get a king, but Shays' Rebellion was probably the most direct catalyst for the convening of the Constitutional Convention in Philadelphia in the spring of 1787, and the little uprising left its fingerprints all over the Constitution.

The traditional view of Shays' Rebellion is that it was a close brush with anarchy that demonstrated the need for a stronger federal government to preserve order and liberty. Along came the Founding Fathers, who gave us just that — the Constitution.

A populist view of the same tale would argue that what the

farmers sought was not anarchy but democracy, both political and economic.

In this view, the issue behind Shays' Rebellion was whether the economic and political system of the new country would be ruled according to the interests of the rich or the poor, the creditors or the debtors, the elite or the masses.

Background of the Rebellion

In the 1770's and 1780's, small farmers composed the majority of the American population. Typically, before the Revolutionary War, they had owned their land, grown their own food and had little contact with money. The few things they needed that they couldn't grow or make themselves, they obtained from small local merchants, often paying in goods or services.

Many of them had neglected their farms to fight in the War for Independence. Shays had been a captain and had fought at Bunker Hill.

Postwar America was mired in an economic depression as it tried to make the transition from English colony to independent trading partner. The English traders who dealt with the big Boston merchants now demanded cash for their goods. In turn, the Boston merchants demanded cash from the small country stores with which they did business. The country merchants passed the demand along to their debtors — the farmers. The farmers found themselves being dragged against their will into a new Boston-based money economy in which they had little interest and poor prospects for survival. They felt their traditional way of life was threatened.

The Boston merchants had lent Massachusetts money to fight the war for independence. They wanted to be repaid in silver and gold so they could do business with their foreign trading partners. And they dominated the politics of the new state. So they got the Legislature to adopt a tax on land (in other words, on farmers) to be paid in gold and silver (which the farmers didn't have).

The tax structure amounted to a transfer of wealth from the taxpayer-farmers to the bondholder-merchants. An estimated one-third of the farmers' income went for taxes.

The farmers also had private debts to the merchants, and the merchants used the courts to collect those debts. Between 1784 and 1786, one-third of the men in Worcester, Mass., were sued for non-payment of debts.

Debtors might lose their farmsteads or be thrown into jail for nonpayment. Most jail inmates in the region were there for failure to pay small debts. In one well-publicized case, Timothy Bigelow, an indebted farmer and Revolutionary War veteran, died in the Worcester prison, where the small, damp cells lacked heat, light and ventilation.

A Change of Yokes

The farmers found themselves asking what they had gained by risking their lives to throw off the yoke of English tyranny, only to find themselves in a new yoke of debt, tended by the Boston merchants and the local courts.

The farmers had gained something by their successful war effort. They now lived in the most democratic society in the world. Although the Constitution wasn't written, each state was a functioning democracy, loosely joined with the other states under the Articles of Confederation.

So the farmers used their new rights to petition the state Legislature, through town meetings and county conventions, for relief. They asked for a law that would restore their right to pay debts in goods and services, or a moratorium on farm foreclosures, or a law that would forgive debts, or — the most popular solution — an issue of paper money that would deflate the currency and provide them some cash to pay their debts. Under the Articles of Confederation, each state had its own monetary system.

Many states had passed paper money laws at the urging of their indebted farmers. But the Massachusetts, sitting in Boston, would not. Eventually, the farmers added to their list of demands, one that the state capital be moved out of Boston.

The Shaysites or Regulators, as they called themselves, moved from petitions to action — although at first the actions were nonviolent. Generally they would surround local courthouses and refuse to let the courts hold sessions that might result in judgments against debtors. In one town, 800 farmers prevented a court session, then freed all those imprisoned for debt.

In a letter to the public in late 1786, Shaysite leader Adam Wheeler said the farmers had "no intention to destroy the public government, but to have the courts suspended to prevent such abuses as have taken place by the sitting of those courts." He said the farmers were "distressed to see valuable members of society dragged from their families to prison."

Respectable Opinion

From the point of view of the merchant and lawyer class, the intimidation of court proceedings and the effort to escape from lawful debts was a direct assault on order, on the legal process and on the right they held to be most fundamental — the right to protect their property.

George Washington himself, in retirement at Mount Vernon, said he was "mortified beyond expression" by the rebellion because it gave the impression in Europe that Americans were incapable of self-government.

Abigail Adams called the farmers "ignorant, restless desperadoes, without conscience or principles (who) have led a deluded multitude to follow their stand, under pretense of grievances which have no existences but in their imaginations."

Connecticut lawyer Noah Webster, he of later dictionary fame, was convinced by the rebellion that democracy didn't work and that a return to monarchy was called for.

"I would sooner be the subject of the caprice of one man than the ignorance of the multitude" he wrote in November of 1786.

The Massachusetts Legislature was so alarmed that it authorized the governor to arrest and imprison without the right of habeas corpus anyone he even suspected was "unfriendly to government."

Spokesmen for the merchant class claimed the farmers sought a total leveling of society and redistribution of all property. Such was never the Shaysites' goal. But as winter set in, their demands became more extreme, such as moving the state capitol from Boston to remove it from the merchants' control.

The King of America

The wildest overreaction was by Nathaniel Gorham, president of the Confederation Congress in 1785-87 and himself a wealthy Massachusetts merchant. To Gorham, as to Webster, the rebellion proved that democracy was impractical. But Gorham went so far as to write to Prince Henry of Prussia in November of 1786 announcing "the failure of our free institutions." He asked the prince if he would be willing to become king of America. The prince replied he wasn't interested because "Americans had shown so much determination against their old king, that they would not readily submit to a new one."

The young government did seem unable to cope. Massachusetts

begged the national government to help, and Congress wanted to. But under the Articles of Confederation, the nation's governing document at the time, the federal government had no standing army and no way to raise money for one.

Governors were supposed to be able to call out state militias. So in September, Massachusetts Gov. James Bowdoin called on the Worcester militia to put down the rebellion. But its members refused. After all, most of the militiamen were small farmers. Some of them joined the Regulators in the court closings.

In January the wealthy Boston merchants took matters into their own hands. Benjamin Lincoln, a Revolutionary War general and a merchant-speculator, called a meeting of some of the richest men in Boston and suggested that if they wanted to save the bulk of their fortunes they'd better invest a small portion of them in the raising and equipping of an army.

Within days, thousands of dollars had been pledged. By late January of 1787 an army was ready to march.

On Jan. 25, 1787, three rebel cadres planned a coordinated attack on the federal arsenal at Springfield, Mass. After arming themselves with the government's guns, they would march to Boston.

Early on the 25th, the leader of one rebel cadre tried to notify Shays that he would not march until the following day. But the messenger was captured by government troops.

At 4 p.m. Shays' troops, unaware of the postponement, marched on the arsenal without support. The attack was repelled. Four farmers were killed and 20 wounded.

From then on it was a mismatch. In two decisive confrontations in February the rebels were routed by government forces. A few dozen farmers were killed. Law and order was restored. Most of the rebels were given amnesty. Shays fled to Vermont, where he found sanctuary.

Three months later, the men who would be known as America's Founding Fathers convened in Philadelphia to frame a new governing document for the young nation.

The Rebellion and the Constitution

Let's pause to put Shays' Rebellion into context as a major factor leading to the Constitutional Convention.

In September of 1786, delegates from five states had met at Annapolis, Md., to deal with trade issues but had decided that the Articles of Confederation prevented them from solving their problems.

The Annapolis Convention ended with a call to all the states to send delegates to Philadelphia the following May.

The call from Annapolis went over with a hollow thud. Congress referred the recommendation to a special committee, then didn't appoint the committee. Most of the state legislatures likewise didn't act on the request that fall.

As word of Shays' Rebellion circulated, however, legislatures started voting to send delegates to Philadelphia. Before the shoot-out at the Springfield arsenal, only five states had done so. In the days immediately after the battle, three more states acted. And on Feb. 21, 1787, 200 years ago last Saturday, Congress belatedly voted to ask the states to send delegates to Philadelphia.

And who were the delegates?

None were women or nonwhites, although in the context of the 1780's that isn't surprising. None were Shaysites. None were small farmers, although that group constituted the biggest portion of the white, male population.

The framers of the Constitution were lawyers, planters, merchants, land speculators, bondholders, creditors. They ranged from the barely rich to the very rich. Historian James McGregor Burns described them as "the well-bred, the well-fed, the well-read and the well-wed." In short, they were members of the class against whom the Shaysites had rebelled.

The document they wrote reflects the fears raised among this class by Shays' Rebellion. For example, the Constitution:

▪ Prohibits states from issuing currency or from making anything other than gold and silver lawful for paying debts.

▪ Authorizes Congress to put down domestic insurrections.

▪ Compels states to turn over fugitives.

▪ Prohibits state laws that impair the sanctity of contracts, so any law forgiving debts would be unconstitutional.

▪ Strengthens the federal government's ability to raise funds — and thus to raise an army should the need arise.

Remember Nathaniel Gorham, the president who had been so panicked by Shays' Rebellion as to declare American democracy a failure? He was a Massachusetts delegate to the Philadelphia convention, was one of the 39 signers of the charter and played a large role at Massachusetts' ratification convention of 1788.

As for Daniel Shays, he eventually was pardoned by Massachusetts, but settled in New York state, where he prospered and became a staunch federalist.

2

A Neglected Source of the Union

The framers of the U.S. Constitution were learned men. Among them were world travelers and world-class scholars who could and did discuss the relative merits of ancient Greek democracy versus the republic of Rome.

They read the latest and greatest European philosophers. They were practical men, some of whom had led the drive for independence. Their political theories had been sharpened in the Continental Congress, the Confederation Congress and the Constitution-writing processes of their states. They were innovators, who borrowed from all these sources and experiences to create a system different from anything that had gone before.

But when the sources of the ideas for the American system are discussed, one important source is usually overlooked:

Indian tribal governments.

Before Columbus "discovered" America, the Five Nations of the Iroquois had formed a confederacy that in some ways provided the model for the centuries-later union of the 13 states.

Canassatego, a leader of the Iroquois Confederation, suggested a union of the 13 colonies. Appropriately, Canassatego made his suggestion on the fourth of July, but the year was 1744, so the *real* Fourth of July hadn't been invented yet. Iroquois leaders had encouraged the colonists since the previous century to unify for purposes of defense and treaty negotiations.

It wasn't just the idea of a union; the nature of the Iroquois system also found its way into the eventual American system.

The ideas of government by the consent of the governed, of checks and balances against centralized authority, that the best government is the least government, that leadership should be by the wise and the virtuous rather than by the well-born, that bad leaders should be impeachable and removable, that all people are born with natural rights, that homes should be safe from unreasonable government intrusions, all of these existed in America before the Europeans came.

The Iroquois system provided for political participation by women, a development the palefaces didn't get around to until 1920. In the Iroquois system, the political leaders (called sachems) were men, but were chosen by women.

Okay, let's not go overboard. The U.S. Constitution was not copied from an Indian tribe.

The Founding Fathers thought of themselves as Englishmen, but they were separated from the mother country by a wide ocean. They shared a continent with the Indians, from whom they were separated only by a thin, movable, imaginary line called the frontier.

They lived between two ancient cultures — their European ancestors and their American neighbors. They were influenced by both.

An Earlier Constitution

The Iroquois Confederation was a constitutional system, based on an oral document called The Great Law of Peace.

We tend to think that white Americans were the first to believe that the leaders of government should be the servants, not the masters of their people. Yet Article 24 of the Great Law enjoins the sachems thusly:

"Their hearts shall be full of peace and good will, and their minds filled with a yearning for the welfare of the people of the League. With endless patience, they shall carry out their duty. Their firmness shall be tempered with a tenderness for their people. Neither anger nor fury shall find lodging in their minds."

The five Iroquois nations were the Seneca, Mohawk, Onondaga, Oneida and Cayuga. Later a sixth, the Tuscarora, joined the confederacy.

In "Forgotten Founders," author Bruce E. Johansen produced strong evidence that the Iroquoian system and the American constitutional system had much in common, and that the tribes provided the source and example for the white founders.

One of the primary conduits for the ideas was Benjamin Franklin, a co-author of the Declaration of Independence, a member of the Constitutional Convention and a veteran ambassador whose first diplomatic assignment was to represent Pennsylvania in talks with the Iroquois.

We tend to think of the frontier of white settlement in this period as a sort of dividing line between light and darkness, between civilization and barbarism, a line that would be crossed only rarely by the bravest souls and then at their peril.

Johansen argues that the frontier was far more permeable, more like a border between two nations. Englishmen and Iroquois crossed it frequently. The Iroquois had towns and buildings and a tradition of hospitality toward visiting whites far more generous than the English had toward the Indians. Among the things that the colonists took with them from their contacts with Indians were ideas about government.

Many English leaders spoke the Iroquois language and many Iroquois leaders spoke English.

Cadwallader Colden, a good friend of Franklin's, wrote the first English description of the Iroquois confederacy, called "History of the Five Nations," published in the 1740's. His description includes the concepts of federalism and government by consent of the governed:

"Each Nation is an absolute Republick by its self, govern'd in all Publick Affairs of War and Peace by the Sachems . . . whose Authority and Power is gain'd by and consists wholly in the Opinion the rest of the Nation have of their Wisdom and Integrity. They never execute their Resolutions by Compulsion or Force upon any of their People. Honour and Esteem are their Principal Rewards, as Shame and being Despised are their Punishments."

Until 1763, the Iroquois, who dominated what is now central New York state and lower Canada, held the balance of power between English settlers on the Atlantic coast and French in the interior and in Canada.

The English needed an alliance with the Iroquois to hold their land against the French and their Indian allies. The colonists and the Iroquois treated each other as sovereign equals and engaged in a series of treaty councils over the middle decades of the 1700's.

The Idea of Union

The Iroquois favored the English against the French, but found it difficult to negotiate treaties because, although the Grand Council of the Iroquois could speak for five nations, the disunited colonies had no mechanism through which to negotiate with one voice.

In the summer of 1744 at Lancaster, Pa., representatives of Pennsylvania, Virginia and Maryland negotiated for two weeks with a large party (245 chiefs, warriors, women and children) representing the Iroquois. On the last day of the meeting, Canassatego, speaker of the Grand Council, told the colonial commissioners:

"Our wise forefathers established union and amity between the Five Nations. This has made us formidable. This has given us great weight and authority with our neighboring Nations. We are a powerful Confederacy and by your observing the same methods our wise forefathers have taken you will acquire much strength and power."

Franklin was not at the meeting, but as a thriving Philadelphia printer he published Canassatego's suggestion in a pamphlet on the colonial-Iroquois treaty council. The Canassatego quote above is from Franklin's pamphlet.

He eventually published 13 accounts of treaty councils with the Iroquois. The pamphlets were good sellers in America and in Europe, where curiosity about the tribes was high.

Franklin took Canassatego's suggestion to heart. In a 1751 letter he wrote:

"It would be a very strange thing if Six Nations of Ignorant Savages should be capable of forming a Scheme for such an Union and be able to execute it in such a manner as that it has subsisted Ages and appears indissoluble, and yet a like Union should be impracticable for ten or a dozen English colonies."

By 1754 he had progressed from publishing Indian treaties to negotiating them himself as a diplomatic representative of Pennsylvania.

That year, serious hostilities with the French began, and the English sought to strengthen their Iroquois alliance at a meeting that came to be called the Albany Congress.

At that meeting Franklin suggested the colonies form a union on the Iroquois model. His plan was adopted by the Albany delegates (representing the New England colonies, New York, Pennsylvania and Maryland) but rejected by the colonial legislatures and ignored by Parliament.

Nevertheless, Franklin remained an unflagging proponent of union, and often mentioned the Iroquois example when arguing his cause.

When the story is told of how the 13 colonies came together, Franklin's role and the Albany Plan of Union are often included. The origins of Franklin's idea are less often mentioned.

He became a lifetime friend, admirer and defender of the Five

Nations risking his own reputation on their behalf in the 1760's.

Jefferson and Indians

Thomas Jefferson wrote a famous letter in 1787, which journalists love to quote because he wrote that if he had to choose between "a government without newspapers or newspapers without a government, I should not hesitate a moment to prefer the latter." (See, I've quoted it again.)

But in a less-famous passage from the same letter, written from Europe, where Jefferson was serving as American minister to France, he wrote:

"I am convinced that those societies, as the Indians, which live without government enjoy in their general mass an infinitely greater degree of happiness than those who live under European governments."

Jefferson's fondness for Indian ways was so strong that on another occasion he wrote: "Indian society may be best, but it is not possible for large numbers of people."

Although Jefferson and Franklin often referred to "savages," they did not mean that the Indians were morally or intellectually inferior to the Europeans. That idea became popular later as part of the rationale for taking the tribal homelands. But Jefferson viewed the Indians as living closer to a state of nature, which, in the thinking of the European Enlightenment, was a good state to live close to.

In the Declaration of Independence in 1776, Jefferson relied on the theory of natural rights, that in a state of nature all men are equal and are endowed by God with certain basic rights, such as the right to life, liberty and the pursuit of happiness.

Jefferson relied on Indian societies for clues about what man was like in a state of nature.

Traditionally his source for this theory is given as John Locke, the English writer who obviously did influence Jefferson.

Although Locke never came to the New World, he had been influenced by the example of the North American tribal governments. We know, because he quoted from it, that Locke read a book published in French in 1636 that described the system by which the Huron Indians of Canada elected their kings, who governed by "consent and persuasion (rather) than by force and compulsion, the public good being the measure of their authority."

A SHORT CONSTITUTIONAL

Benjamin Franklin, one of our most beloved founders, framers and all-around sages, was voted out of the Pennsylvania colonial Assembly in 1764 for being an Indian lover.

After more than a decade of Indian diplomacy, Franklin had developed fondness, admiration and loyalty toward the Indians, especially those who had helped the English win the French and Indian War.

The same was not true of the Western Pennsylvania frontiersmen whose hunger for Indian land could not wait for new treaty negotiations.

On Dec. 14, 1763, 57 white vigilantes raided a peaceable settlement of Conestoga (one of the Iroquois nations), killing six of the 20 Indians living there. Two weeks later, more than 200 vigilantes raided the jail in Lancaster, Pa., where the remaining 14 Conestogas had been taken for protection, smashed in the door and killed the Indians.

The outraged Franklin responded with a pamphlet demanding punishment for the killers, whom he called "Christian White Savages."

Word reached Philadelphia that the vigilantes' next strike would be against an Indian encampment near the city.

Franklin raised a militia of almost 1,000 men and rode west to face down the frontiersmen. He succeeded, probably saving about 140 Indian lives, but by his actions "made myself many enemies among the populace," who were not as sympathetic to the Indians. And sure enough, the leading citizen of Philadelphia was defeated that year for reelection to the colonial Assembly.

3

A Little Guy Named Madison

If James Madison had a better publicity agent, we'd have to make room for him on Mount Rushmore.

After all, Madison is the man whom historians call the "father of the U.S. Constitution," one of our two sacred national documents.

He was one of the early agitators for the Constitutional Convention of 1787, the first to arrive in Philadelphia, and a key player during the deliberations. During the campaign for ratification he figured prominently in two of the most difficult and crucial states. After ratification, he shepherded through Congress the first 10 amendments, which constitute the Bill of Rights.

During 1987, the year of the constitutional bicentennial, Madison figured to finally take his place among the major demigods of American history. He was mentioned prominently in the bicentennial hoopla.

Yet Madison still seems to muddle along in middling obscurity — one of those names we can identify as an early president, but that's about it.

In a Wall Street Journal/NBC poll, only 1 percent of respondents identified Madison as the one who played the biggest role in the creation of the Constitution.

(The "winner" in the poll was Madison's friend Thomas Jefferson, who was named by 31 percent as the primary author of the Constitution, a neat trick for someone who was in France during the entire convention. Jefferson was, of course, the primary author of the Declaration of Independence, the other sacred document of our founding. He's already on Mt. Rushmore.)

Madison's relative obscurity points up one of the characteristics of American politics and culture — our preference for personality over issues, for style over substance.

Madison's problem is that he was all substance. As the architect of and campaign manager for the Constitution, he was brilliant.

But in providing material for popular legend, he was a big zero. Neither his personality nor his biography include the kind of appealing qualities or dramatic events that help historical figures stick in the public mind.

A Hard Image to Sell

History is kind to war heroes. Madison played no military role in the War for Independence. As president (1809-1817) he did get us into a war, but it was the unpopular and inglorious War of 1812. Madison's best-remembered act was to flee Washington when the English took the city and burned the White House and the Capitol.

The mythmaking machinery favors guys who split rails and pull themselves up from poverty. Madison was born to wealth, attended Princeton University (back then it was the College of New Jersey), owned slaves and never had to work for a living. In no legend does he kill a bear or chop down a cherry tree.

Although he wrote and argued cogently and seems to have been an obsessive notetaker, he never emitted witty epigrams like Ben Franklin nor heroic quotable quotes like his political enemy Patrick Henry.

Madison liked to dress in black, a better color for bankers, undertakers or villains than for heroes of history. His voice was faint. He worried incessantly about his health, which was frail. He feared women, married late, and fathered no children.

The only thing he managed to father was a little old document that has lasted 200 years as our mythic beacon of liberty, guarantor of freedom, magic talisman of democracy and argument settler of last resort.

Before we get too carried away, let's make clear that the writing, ratifying and amending of the Constitution was not a one-man show.

A convention of 55 men wrote the Constitution in Philadelphia in the summer of 1787. While other delegates came and went, Madison was present every day. He was active and influential, but he didn't dominate.

In fact, Madison lost several battles during the convention. He favored a stronger federal government. He wanted Congress to have the power to strike down state laws. He wanted both the House and Senate to be apportioned according to population. And he wanted the president and some number of Supreme Court justices to form a "Council of Revision" that would have absolute veto power over all acts of Congress.

Having lost on all of these points, he wrote despondently to Jefferson in France:

"I hazard an opinion nevertheless that the plan (the Constitution), should it be adopted, will neither effectually answer its national object (nor) prevent the local mischiefs which everywhere excite disgusts against the state governments."

But the creation of the Constitution took more than those four months in Philadelphia. Madison's claim to paternity rests as much on his contributions before and after the convention.

The Nationalists

The calling of the Constitutional Convention was no accident, nor was it an idea that bubbled up from ordinary citizens. It required scheming and coordination by a small group of men who believed that the 13 states must be governed as one nation and would require a stronger central government than was set up by the Articles of Confederation. Madison was among the earliest and most energetic of these men, who are called the nationalists.

Their views were held by a small minority of the population. In the post-war euphoria of independence, most Americans didn't view themselves as Americans at all. Their primary loyalty was to their states. The loose connection of the states under the Articles of Confederation, with no national executive or judiciary, seemed best designed to preserve their new-found freedoms.

But the economic depression of the 1780's seemed to suggest the need for some kind of central coordination or regulation of interstate commerce. The political troubles of 1786-87, most notably Shays Rebellion, suggested the need for a national political structure and an executive who could act quickly in an emergency. In these conditions, the nationalists saw an opportunity to advance their cause.

What follows is a summary of some of the ways Madison helped plant and nurture this which became the Constitution.

■ Madison helped engineer the calling of the Annapolis Convention in September of 1786 and helped write the report of that convention, which ended with a call for all the states to send delegates to Philadelphia in May 1787. The Philadelphia meeting became what we now call the Constitutional Convention.

■ Madison, only 36 in 1787, crafted the plan that became the basis for the early discussions at the convention. The plan was crucial because, instead of suggesting a few amendments to the Articles of Confederation, as the convention was supposed to do, it called for scrapping the articles and replacing them with a new charter. The plan is sometimes called the Virginia Plan, sometimes the Randolph Plan, sometimes the Big States Plan, but never the Madison Plan.

■ That's because, in a typical Madison move, he recruited Edmund Randolph to present the plan. This had a double advantage of associating the plan with the influential Randolph, governor of Virginia, the biggest state, and of drawing Randolph, who was not a thoroughgoing nationalist, further into Madison's camp. (Randolph ended up refusing to sign the Constitution, but supported it during the ratification debate in Virginia.)

■ During the convention, Madison was an active participant. He spoke 161 times, second most of any member. (Gouverneur Morris of Pennsylvania, the convention's most frequent speechifier, draftsman of most of the Constitution, and the only member with a wooden leg, is another key framer whose name hasn't made much of a dent in popular lore. "Gouverneur," by the way, was his name, not his office.)

■ Characteristically, Madison also took the most complete notes, although he didn't allow them to be published until after his death. The convention kept no official record of its debates, the meetings were closed to press and public and the members were sworn to secrecy. Thanks to Madison, historians have their best information on the discussions.

■ As soon as the convention was over, Madison, who was also a member of the Confederation Congress, headed for New York, where Congress met, to lobby successfully for a resolution referring the charter to the states for ratification.

■ As the battle over ratification began, Madison remained a key figure, helping set strategy for the overall ratification efforts and playing a major role in two of the most difficult and critical states, Virginia and New York.

■ At the Virginia ratification convention he led the pro-Constitution forces on the floor and took the heat from the popular and eloquent Patrick Henry. Henry assailed the Constitution daily as an aristocratic document. Madison, with his wealthy background and effete manners, made a perfect target for Henry's thunderous denunciations. But the Constitution squeaked through.

■ New York was a bastion of anti-Constitution sentiment. Its popular governor, George Clinton, opposed ratification. Madison's role was as one of the authors of the famous Federalist Papers, which were first published in New York newspapers as letters favoring ratification. The Papers, which include contributions by Alexander Hamilton and John Jay, are considered by some to be America's greatest contribution to political theory. They were published under a pseudonym, Publius. New York ratified by a narrow margin.

■ Madison had opposed the inclusion of a Bill of Rights in the Constitution, arguing that it wasn't necessary. His viewpoint prevailed at the convention, but several key states ratified after being promised that such guarantees of rights would be considered as amendments by the first Congress. Madison was the leader of the House in that Congress and, although he privately called it a "nauseous project," he sponsored the amendments that became the Bill of Rights.

Madison finally married, in 1798, the likable Dolly Payne Todd, who became famous as a Washington partygiver. Along with Jefferson, he helped form the first opposition party in American history. (The Constitution, by the way, makes no mention of political parties.) He was Jefferson's secretary of state (1801-1809), defeated one of his fellow framers, C.C. Pinckney of South Carolina, for the presidency (1808), served two terms and outlived every other member of the Constitutional Convention. He died in 1836 at the age of 85.

4

What Was the Framers' Vision?

From a distance of 200 years, through a haze of myth and embellishment, the Constitutional Convention of 1787 is hard to see clearly.

Were the framers wise and virtuous giants who walked the earth? In this heroic view, the framers were divinely inspired visionaries who, in a time of crisis, rose above petty self-interest to bequeath a majestic system of government and commerce, rights and liberties, checks and balances, and to propel a young nation along an unstoppable trajectory to greatness.

Or were they fat cats and aristocrats who conspired in Philadelphia to favor the rich over the poor, decrease democracy while pretending to promote it, and impose property rights and elitism as the supreme law of the land?

Or were they farsighted, practical politicians who knew how to make the deals necessary to resolve conflicts between big-staters and small-staters; slaveholders and anti-slavers?

Okay, enough questions. Cue the drum roll. May we have the envelope, please. The answers are:

Yes, yes and yes.

The framers *were* visionaries trying to create a society of prosperity and grandeur. They *were* self-serving aristocrats making sure that their own class would be sheltered from the danger — ever present in a democracy — that common people would actually try to run things. They *were* wheeler-dealers who made compromises — some clever, some repugnant — to get a charter.

And they were something more. They were nationalists, which in their time meant they favored strengthening the national government at the expense of the states. In 1987 it may be hard to picture, but in 1787 America, that was a radical position.

Most Americans felt primary loyalty to their states. Central authority was viewed as a slippery step on the slide toward tyranny. In a way, the War for Independence was a war against central authority, against being governed from a far-off place.

The Articles of Confederation, which laid out the system of government that the Constitution replaced, reflected this fear. Written during the war, it did not form the 13 states into a large nation. In its own words, it created "a firm league of friendship" among 13 independent states and provided a framework for cooperation so the states could defend themselves, trade with each other and present a somewhat united front in international matters.

The nationalists at Philadelphia knew their point of view would frighten many of their countrymen. That's why they called themselves Federalists instead of nationalists during the campaign for ratification.

In fact, the framers went out of their way to leave the word "nation" out of the Constitution to appease those who feared it. But semantics couldn't mask one of their guiding purposes — to create a nation out of 13 quarrelsome and diverse sovereign states.

The heroic view of the framers is, if you'll pardon the expression, one of the myths that bind us. We don't really *think* 55 bewigged guys could be as wise and virtuous as this fable requires, but sometimes, when the wind blows through the flag just right, we *feel* it might be so.

The Framers as Aristocrats

The view of the framers as self-serving aristocrats, while unappealing from a patriotic perspective, can't be dismissed lightly. Most of the founders had a personal economic stake in the outcome of the convention.

Of the 55 delegates at the convention, 40 owned government bonds that had depreciated dramatically under the Articles of Confederation, and soared in value after the Constitution required the new federal government to pay them off.

Twenty-four of the framers were money-lenders. The Constitution, by ensuring the sanctity of contracts and centralizing control of the money supply, shored up the value of their loan portfolios.

At least 16 owned slaves. The Constitution improved the legal and political position of slaveholders. Many owned land in the Western territories. A strong central government was a key to making those investments pay off.

All were members of the upper class — George Washington was one of the richest man in America — and that class did well in the aftermath of the convention and has prospered ever since.

The theory also fits much of the rhetoric at the convention. The framers spoke of democracy as a menace and of the masses as untrustworthy.

Roger Sherman, one of those important but oft-forgotten authors of the Constitution, expressed a view echoed by many at the convention when he said: "The people immediately should have as little to do as may be about the Government. They (lack) information and are constantly liable to be misled."

The framers paid great attention to securing the rights of property against the passions of the masses. George Mason of Virginia proposed a property-owning qualification for the Senate. James Madison proposed nine-year terms, so that senators could be shielded from democratic pressure. Two South Carolina delegates wanted the relative wealth of states to be reflected in their power in Congress.

The Framers as Compromisers

The third view, that of a convention of practical politicians, modernizes the framers. They may have worn three-cornered hats and spelled funnye, but they were political men making a political system and they did it the way it is done now. They represented their constituencies, negotiated with representatives of other constituencies and compromised until everyone was satisfied.

The two big fights that threatened to tear the convention apart were between large and small states over voting power in Congress, and between the Southern and Northern states over how slaves should be counted.

Things got so tense that Washington wrote in a letter: "I almost despair of seeing a favorable issue to the proceedings of the Convention, and do therefore repent having had any agency in the business." The remark sheds an interesting light on Washington's situation.

He was the most famous and revered American of his time, and he believed in the nationalists' vision. The other nationalists knew his presence was crucial to their cause and worked hard to get a reluctant Washington to come to Philadelphia. Why was he so reluctant? He had personal and business reasons for wanting to spend that summer at home in Mount Vernon, but he also wanted to be very careful not to invest his unblemished reputation in what might turn out to be an unsuccessful cause.

The Connecticut Compromise

The deadlock between large and small states was broken by the so-called Connecticut Compromise, which called for equal representation for the states in the Senate and representation based on population in the House.

In the argument over slavery, Southern delegates wanted slaves included in the population counts that determined the size of House delegations. Northerners wanted no credit given. Delegates from the Deep South also wanted assurances that Congress would allow the slave trade to continue.

In the compromise that settled these issues, a slave would be counted as three-fifths of a person and the slave trade would be beyond the reach of the federal government, but only until 1808.

These tradeoffs show the pragmatic side of the founders. But by focusing on a few issues dividing the group, the pragmatic view distracts from an understanding of what the framers were really after — nationhood.

The word "national" was in a paragraph adopted early in the convention but was later deleted because it would be too explosive. In 1787, many Americans thought of "national" the way many today view "communist."

Those who feared national government believed that a republican form of government worked only in small units. In large units, the government got too far from the people; the people couldn't watch the rulers closely enough; the rulers lost their identification with their constituents; armies got too big, and some form of despotism, either monarchy or aristocracy, set in.

The opponents of the Constitution were those who held that fear. Some were present at the convention, but several left in disgust when the general trend was established. The convention was therefore in the hands of nationalists. With their nationalism in mind, the other three views of the framers come into clearer focus.

The Framers as Nationalists

Yes, they were visionaries, but their vision was not of rights and liberties. (The convention rejected a bill of rights 10 states to 0.

The Bill of Rights was added later by amendment.) They envisioned the nation that a strong central government might forge out of the 13 states and the huge Western territory.

A government with power to regulate commerce (no such power previously existed) and with a judiciary to settle interstate disputes (the Articles had none) could become the engine of prosperity.

Yes, the founders were self-serving aristocrats, and a strong national government was their mechanism. With taxing power (the Confederation Congress had none), a government could pay off the bonds they held. A government authorized to maintain a standing army (the Confederation was not) could continue to push the Indians west.

In an individual state, demagogues might seize the passions of the uninformed masses. It had happened in Rhode Island, where the debtors were in control, and almost had happened in Massachusetts during Shays' Rebellion. But in a national legislature, men of substance and education (read wealth) were bound to predominate.

As compromising pragmatists, they had nationalism as their goal. Why should large-state members agree to a Senate in which their populations gave them no advantage? Why should Northerners agree to the three-fifths rule, which, in effect, gave free Southerners more representation in the House than free Northerners? Because those were the deals they had to make to get the national government that would fulfill both their selfish and their unselfish visions.

Gouverneur Morris of Pennsylvania, another key member of the convention, put the details of the compromises in perspective on the day he signed the proposed Constitution, saying:

"The moment this plan goes forth, all other considerations will be laid aside and the great question will be: Shall there be a *national* government or not? And this must take place or a general anarchy will be the alternative."

A SHORT CONSTITUTIONAL

A potpourri about the constitutional convention of 1787:

■ Most of the delegates were late for the convention. The convention was scheduled to begin May 14, but it was May 25 before a bare quorum of seven states enabled work to begin.

The New Hampshire delegation was nine weeks late, arriving after most issues had been settled.

∎ George Washington presided, but took almost no part in the discussions, indicating approval or disapproval of suggestions with a smile or a frown.

∎ One state — Rhode Island — never sent a delegation to Philadelphia. Of the 12 states participating, several delegations came late or left early or came and went during the convention. As a result, when most of the key votes were taken, about 10 of the states were present and voting.

∎ Of 74 delegates selected, only 55 ever came to the convention and of those, more than a dozen drifted away before the end. Only 39 men signed the proposed constitution.

∎ Three prominent delegates stayed to the end but refused to sign. Elbridge Gerry of Massachusetts said the Constitution would be too divisive. George Mason of Virginia listed a number of objections, primarily the lack of a bill of rights. Gov. Edmund Randolph of Virginia, sponsor of the plan on which much of the final document was based, said he had to keep his options open in case he decided to oppose the Constitution at the Virginia ratifying convention. He ended up supporting it.

∎ More than half of the delegates, 34 out of 55, were lawyers, although many did not practice law for a living. It was a young assemblage. Average age: 41. The youngest member, Jonathan Dayton of New Jersey, was 26. Alexander Hamilton was 32; James Madison, 36; Gouverneur Morris, 35. Oldest member: Ben Franklin, 81.

∎ The convention was closed to the press and public. The members were sworn to secrecy about the deliberations. Madison, who took the most complete set of notes about the proceedings, did not allow them to be published until after his death in 1836.

∎ The convention far exceeded its mandate. The resolution of the Confederation Congress asking states to send delegates to Philadelphia said the convention was "for the sole and express purpose of revising the Articles of Confederation," not to throw out the articles and replace them with an entirely new document as the convention did.

∎ The framers "cheated" on the ratification of the Constitution. Under the Articles of Confederation, amendments had to be approved by all 13 states. Any amendments the convention might have proposed should have been put to the same test. With Rhode Island boycotting the proceedings and New York controlled by anti-federalists, it was unlikely anything produced at Philadelphia would have received unanimous approval.

So the framers adopted Article VII, the last and shortest of the original Constitution, which said if any nine states ratified, the Constitution would create a federation of at least those nine. The trick worked. By the time New York and Rhode Island ratified, the new republic was already formed and they had to choose between getting on board or becoming independent nations.

5

The Man on the $10 Bill

"The voice of the people has been said to be the voice of God," Alexander Hamilton told the Constitutional Convention on June 18, 1787. "However generally this maxim has been quoted and believed, it is not true in fact. The people are turbulent and changing. They seldom judge or determine right."

He proceeded during a six-hour diatribe to outline the Hamilton plan for the government of the United States, featuring minimal democracy, a president with a life term and king-like powers (Hamilton referred to him as a monarch), an aristocratic Senate (also elected for life) and the reduction of the states to hollow appendages of the supreme national government with their governors appointed by the president-king.

How, you may be wondering, did this guy get his face on the $10 bill?

The irony of Alexander Hamilton is that a person with such attitudes contributed so substantially to the launching of the American republic. The irony is well-illustrated by his connection with the U.S. Constitution. He helped get the convention called and helped write the charter, but on the day he signed it he expressed his disappointment with it.

Then he wrote about it as if it was God's gift to good government, worked to get it adopted (including telling a giant, barefaced lie on the floor of the New York ratifying convention) and shortly before his death confessed that he had always considered it a "frail and worthless fabric."

Hamilton also has the questionable distinction of being the only signer of the Constitution to die in a duel.

Brilliant, arrogant, fearless and socially ambitious, Hamilton had risen from an illegitimate birth in the West Indies to become a Columbia University graduate, a successful lawyer and a member by marriage of one of New York's richest and most respectable families.

He was a Revolutionary War hero, serving as Gen. George Washington's aide and leading a charge at the key battle of Yorktown.

Hamilton despised the Articles of Confederation, the decentralized form of government under which the 13 states were governed from 1781 to 1788. Even before the Articles were ratified, he agitated for a stronger central government.

Hamilton attended the Annapolis Convention of 1786, and wrote its final report, which called for the Constitutional Convention.

The New York governor, George Clinton, an opponent of national government, allowed his political enemy Hamilton to be one of New York's delegates to Philadelphia, but Clinton surrounded him with two anti-nationalists, Robert Yates and John Lansing.

Picture the New York delegation at the convention: Yates and Lansing steaming because every suggestion is too nationalist for them, Hamilton steaming because nothing is nationalist enough.

Hamilton's Big Speech

Hamilton sat through four weeks of the convention saying little. Then on June 18, he boiled over with his big speech. In his written notes, Hamilton had even gone the final step, suggesting that the American monarchy be made hereditary, but he apparently knew better than to mention it on the floor.

He did, according to one notetaker's version of the speech, argue that the people themselves "begin to be tired of an excess of democracy" under the Articles of Confederation. Even the plan favored by the other nationalist delegates was nothing but "pork still, with a little change of the sauce."

He had taken the floor at the beginning of the day and yielded it back at the end. No one had interrupted, nor asked a question nor offered an argument.

They just adjourned, retired to their quarters, and the next day resumed as if Hamilton's plan had never been offered.

Hamilton stayed 11 more days, then went home, missing most of the crucial final votes. Yates and Lansing also departed in disgust, leaving New York unrepresented.

Hamilton returned in time to sign the proposed Constitution, saying as he did so that "no man's ideas are more remote from the plan than my own are known to be. But is it possible to deliberate between anarchy and convulsion on one side, and the chance of good to be expected from the plan on the other?"

Hamilton's claim to being at least an uncle or maybe father-in-law of the Constitution is secured by his activities after the convention.

First he coordinated and co-authored (with James Madison and John Jay) the famed Federalist Papers, 85 essays explaining and glorifying the Constitution as a near perfect charter.

The papers now read as if they were written to impress political science professors and annoy high school students, but they actually were published in mass circulation newspapers in New York as propaganda for ratification.

If Hamilton was expressing his true feelings at the convention, the Federalist Papers wildly exaggerate his enthusiasm for the Constitution.

At the New York ratifying convention, Hamilton and Jay led the pro-ratification forces. Hamilton appeared in his role as Federalist author, praising the Constitution as a perfect balancer of democracy and stability, of state and federal power.

The Big Lie

Hamilton held forth along these lines one day during the New York convention when Lansing, his old adversary, rose to ask a question.

How, Lansing wanted to know, did Hamilton square his current rhetoric with his opinion, expressed in the big speech in Philadelphia, that state and federal authority could not co-exist and the states should be done away with?

Hamilton offered an interesting explanation for this apparent contradiction. He denied he ever said any such thing.

The Philadelphia convention had been closed to the press and the members were sworn to secrecy about the debates. Lansing had no way to prove his assertion.

By 1840, when publication of Madison's notes from the convention proved that Hamilton had been lying, all parties to the dispute were safely in their graves.

After ratification, Hamilton became Washington's secretary of treasury. His fiscal program fulfilled the constitutional promise of paying off the war bonds (many of which were held by his fellow framers). He also structured the first national tax program and proposed the first national bank.

In 1800, when Thomas Jefferson and Aaron Burr received the same number of electoral votes, Hamilton helped throw the presidency to Jefferson. He clashed with Burr again over the latter's campaign for governor of New York. Offended by Hamilton's remarks about him, Burr challenged Hamilton to a duel. Hamilton accepted. Burr fatally shot him July 11, 1804.

Not long before the duel, he had written to one of his fellow framers:

"Perhaps no man in the United States has sacrificed or done more for the present Constitution than myself; and contrary to all my anticipations ... I am still laboring to prop the frail and worthless fabric."

6

The Roads Not Taken

Alexander Hamilton's proposal for an elective monarchy met with deafening silence at the Constitutional Convention. Here are some of the other proposals considered but not adopted:

How Many Presidents at a Time?

The idea of one man heading the executive branch of the government, appointing the judicial branch and commanding the military scared the dickens out of some members of the convention, who considered it all too easy for a president to crown himself king.

"Do the gentlemen mean to pave the way to hereditary monarchy?" asked Virginia's George Mason in alarm.

Mason and Edmund Randolph favored a three-member executive, with one member representing the North, one the South and one the middle states.

To prevent the executive from dominating the Supreme Court, William Livingston of New Jersey suggested letting the chief justice appoint the other members of the Supreme Court.

President Plutocrat

A number of delegates wanted to make sure that this powerful executive would be a member of the proper class. Ben Franklin and others suggested constitutionally banning a salary for the president. That way, only a man of independent wealth could afford to take the job.

Charles Pinckney of South Carolina offered a more direct solution. He wanted the U.S. Constitution to specify that the president had to have a net worth of at least $100,000.

Even Before the New Hampshire Primary?

The Electoral College method of electing the president was a mishmash of various strategies that were discussed.

The original Virginia Plan, proposed at the beginning of the convention, called for the people to elect the House, the House to elect the Senate and the whole Congress to elect the president.

The convention considered allowing the governors of the states to pick the president. James Wilson of Pennsylvania trusted the people to elect him directly. After the Electoral College idea took hold, Wilson suggested that the electors could be chosen by lot from the members of Congress. He was kidding.

Seven More Years

The Virginia Plan included a seven-year term for the president, who would then be ineligible for re-election. This was adopted early in the convention, as was a three-year term for House members. James Madison favored both of those provisions and a nine-year term for senators. Annual elections for members of the House, considered the most democratic suggestion, was favored by Wilson.

Thomas Jefferson, reviewing the Constitution from Paris where he was the American ambassador, thought one of the biggest mistakes the convention made was allowing the president to serve more than one term. He felt that once in office, no president could be defeated for re-election and the job would end up lasting for life and developing the tone of a monarchy. He was wrong, of course. Only one president in our history (Franklin D. Roosevelt) ever served a third term or even ran for one. Four presidents in the 20th century alone have been defeated for re-election. (William H. Taft in 1912; Herbert Hoover in 1932; Gerald Ford in 1976 and Jimmy Carter in 1980.) Still, Jefferson would probably be reassured by the 22nd Amendment, which limits a president to two terms.

Sen. Moneybags

If the U.S. Senate has a reputation as a millionaires' club, that would be okay with Founding Father C.C. Pinckney (the cousin of Charles Pinckney). He said at the convention that since the Senate was "meant to represent the wealth of the country, it ought to be composed of persons of wealth. And if no allowance (salary) was to be made the wealthy alone would undertake the service." George Mason of Virginia favored a minimum property requirement for senators.

Pay Now, Vote Later

Oliver Ellsworth of Connecticut wanted only those who paid taxes to vote in federal elections. The more common suggestion was limiting the vote to landowners or establishing a property qualification.

Gouverneur Morris of Pennsylvania led the charge for that idea, saying: "Give the votes to people who have no property and they will sell them to the rich, who will be able to buy them.

"Children do not vote. Why? because they (lack) prudence, because they have no will of their own. The ignorant and the dependent (meaning those who depend on employers for their incomes) can be as little trusted."

Although the Constitution did not impose a national property requirement for voting, it left the question up to the states. Most had property requirements for voting in state elections.

Veto This, Wise Guy

Veto power was kicked around a great deal before the delegates compromised on a presidential veto that could be overridden by two-thirds of both houses. The Virginia Plan called for a special Council of Revision, composed of the president and some members of the judiciary, which would have absolute veto power.

The plan also empowered Congress to veto state laws. The convention at first adopted that provision, which Madison felt was urgently needed. When the convention reversed the earlier vote, Madison was terribly discouraged.

State of the States

The issue of state-federal relations, and of the relative power of small states, was a powder keg threatening the whole project. Most of those who favored a strong national government knew that the country wasn't ready for too much power to be transferred at once from the states. But George Read of Delaware threw caution to the winds, proclaiming, "The state governments must be swept away," and the whole country governed from the Capitol.

The New Jersey Plan, suggested by William Paterson of that state, called for a one-house legislature in which each state would have equal voting power. When the big states continued to insist that population be reflected, David Brearly, also of New Jersey, said the way to make such a plan fair was that "a map of the United States be spread out, that all the existing boundaries be erased and that a new partition of the whole be made in thirteen equal parts."

7

Ratification by Hook
and by Crook

In Pennsylvania they had to drag two legislators literally kicking
and screaming to the statehouse. In Massachusetts they had to
flatter and bamboozle the governor. In Virginia they had to wait
for the greatest talker of the times to run out of things to say. They
conquered New York with a threat of encirclement and dismem-
berment. And in Rhode Island — well, Rhode Island just went
porcupine on them.

"They" were the backers of the proposed new U.S. Constitution
in 1787 and 1788. The events refer to some of the tactics and
incidents that occurred during the battle over ratification.

Because the Constitution has been revered by Americans during
most of the past 200 years, it's easy to fall into the habit of
thinking it was enthusiastically received by a grateful nation as
soon as it had fallen from the pens of the Founding Fathers.

On the contrary, when the framers signed the Constitution on
Sept. 17, 1787, and adjourned the Philadelphia convention, the
battle was just beginning. The charter was nothing but a proposal
until at least nine states ratified it.

The framers had asked each state to hold a specially elected
convention to decide on ratification. This method would help
justify the grand opening of the preamble — "We the People" —
but it also had tactical advantages.

Most of the power of the new federal government would come at
the expense of state power. Asking the legislatures to ratify would
be asking them to diminish their own power.

Almost three years passed between adjournment in Philadelphia
and the final, reluctant ratification in porcupiney Rhode Island.
Six states ratified quickly and by wide margins; the other six with
varying degrees of trouble, controversy and hijinks.

What follows are brief summaries of the action and argument in some of the difficult states.

Pennsylvania

Pro-ratification forces (who came to be known as federalists) in the Pennsylvania Assembly knew they had enough votes to call for a ratifying convention. But when the bill came up on Sept. 28, 1787, the day before the assembly was required to adjourn, the assembly was two members short of a quorum.

The reason for the shortage was soon revealed. Nineteen anti-ratification assemblymen had locked themselves in their lodgings to forestall a vote until the next session.

Early the next morning, a mob smashed windows and broke down the door of a house where some of the "antis" were huddled, grabbed two assemblymen and, in modern parlance, made them an offer they couldn't refuse. The mob dragged them to the statehouse and deposited them in their seats.

The motion for a ratification convention passed 45 to (not surprisingly) two. At the convention Dec. 12, 1787, Pennsylvania ratified by 46-23. (Delaware was first, ratifying unanimously on Dec. 7.) Three more easy ratifications (New Jersey, Georgia and Connecticut) followed in December of 1787 and January of 1788.

Massachusetts

The federalists feared Massachusetts. Boston, controlled by rich merchants, was strong for the Constitution. But West-Central Massachusetts, where Shays Rebellion of the previous year had left a residue of anger toward the wealthy, was a hotbed of anti-federalism.

Delegate Amos Singletry, a farmer and revolutionary veteran, gave a general sense of how the "antis" viewed the Constitution:

"These lawyers and men of learning and moneyed men that talk so finely and gloss over matters so smoothly to make us poor illiterate people swallow down the pill expect to get into Congress themselves. They expect to be the managers of this Constitution and get all the power and all the money into their own hands and then they will swallow up us little fellows like the great Leviathan, Mr. President; yes, just as the whale swallowed up Jonah."

Then, as now, money carried some political influence, and the federalists had the deep pockets. When one of the Boston newspapers attacked the Constitution, federalist readers and advertisers boycotted it.

The anti-federalists had started the convention with enough votes to reject the Constitution, but by late January, the federalists believed they could win if they could bring around John Hancock.

Hancock, governor of Massachusetts and presiding officer at the convention, was said to have influence over about 50 delegates. He was inclined against ratification, but had avoided taking a clear public position.

At a secret meeting with Hancock, the federalist leaders moved in for the clincher.

They flattered Hancock, telling him only he could save the republic. They offered him glory. They had prepared nine amendments that they wanted to recommend to be added to the Constitution after ratification. They asked Hancock to sponsor the nine amendments.

And they invented what has now become a long and distinguished American tradition of co-opting a politician by dangling a place on the national ticket.

Everyone assumed that George Washington of Virginia would be the first president. But wouldn't he need a New Englander as vice president to, in effect, balance the ticket? And wouldn't the obvious choice be the great Bostonian friend of liberty Hancock, especially if he became the hero of the ratification?

And what if Virginia didn't join the union? If Washington never became eligible, how could the country do better than the man whose John Hancock was synonymous with the Declaration of Independence?

Hancock bit. When the motion for ratification was made, he introduced the amendments, claiming to have conceived them himself, and endorsed ratification. (The following year, a Massachusetts man was indeed elected vice president. His name was John Adams.)

It turned out that every tactic had been necessary. Ratification passed Feb. 6, 1788, by 187-168.

One young lawyer who had been explicitly instructed by his constituents to vote "no" voted "yes," saying he trusted that they would forgive him. He was wrong. The reaction at home convinced him to move to another town.

Maryland ratified in April, South Carolina in May, giving the federalists eight states.

Virginia

"This paper is the most fatal plan that could possibly be conceived to enslave a free people," said Patrick Henry at the Virginia ratifying convention. He was talking about our Constitution.

He predicted that the charter would be the death of liberty because it lacked a bill of rights, established the aristocracy as supreme and discarded the principles of a confederation of states in favor of an overly centralized national government.

The union had to have Virginia, the oldest, biggest, richest state. It would provide four of the first five presidents. But first, the federalists had to get past Henry.

The pro-ratifiers had some heavy hitters on their side. Future President James Madison, the father of the Constitution, was there; so was Virginia Gov. Edmund Randolph, who would become the first U.S. attorney general; and John Marshall, who would be the first great chief justice. But they had no spellbinder to match Henry.

"Liberty, the greatest of earthly possessions," he said one day during the ratifying convention in June of 1788, "give us that precious jewel and you may take everything else. But I am fearful I have lived long enough to become an old-fashioned fellow. (He was only 52.) Perhaps an invincible attachment to the dearest rights of man may, in these refined, enlightened days, be deemed old-fashioned; if so, I am contented to be so."

The Constitution gave away too much power to the distant central government, he said. Why such a vast transfer of states' rights all at once? "If you give too little power today, you may give more tomorrow .... But if you give too much power today ... tomorrow will never come."

Henry spoke at least once on 18 days of the 23-day convention. One day he spoke for seven solid hours — thundering, whispering, joking, pleading.

"The rights of conscience, trial by jury, liberty of the press, all your immunities and franchises, all pretensions to human rights and privileges are rendered insecure by this change," Henry warned.

His description of the handcuffing of liberties under the Constitution was so vivid that, according to legend, one delegate clutched at his wrists, as if to make sure the manacles weren't already in place.

Madison, the federalist floor leader, was master of the theory behind the Constitution, but lacked the voice or style to give it life. Still he bore the burden of answering Henry.

By the end it was clear that the framers had blundered by leaving out a bill of rights and that one would have to be added. The question was whether to amend before ratification, as Henry urged, or ratify first and amend later, as the federalists advocated.

"Does it not insult your judgment," Henry demanded, "to tell you: Adopt first, and then amend!"

Henry's motion to demand prior amendments failed 88-80. Madison's motion to ratify with recommended amendments passed 89-79 on June 25. Virginia was in, thinking it had been the decisive ninth state. Later news showed that New Hampshire had ratified four days earlier.

Ten states were in. The Constitution was in effect. But what would the union be without New York?

New York

New York had seemed one of the surest states to reject ratification. Although New York City was strong for the Constitution, the rest of the state was so strongly opposed that the anti-federalists started the convention with a 46-19 advantage.

The anti leaders, in coordination with the anti-federalists in Virginia, planned to ratify conditionally, calling for amendments first, as Patrick Henry advocated. Even if nine other states ratified, the nation could not go forward without two of its biggest states.

But when the news arrived that Virginia had ratified unconditionally, the opposition was thrown into disarray. If New York rejected the Constitution, it might have to exist as a separate nation.

That's when Alexander Hamilton, the federalist floor leader in New York, dropped his bomb. New York City clearly wanted to join the new constitutional union. If New York state wanted to, in effect, secede from its sister states, Hamilton hinted, the delegates should bear in mind that New York City might decide to secede from the state, leaving the nation of New York without its seaport and major city.

That was a chance many of the anti-federalists were unwilling to take. As in Massachusetts, a number of delegates violated instructions from their constituents. An additional number — just enough — abstained. The Constitution was ratified by 30-27.

North Carolina, Rhode Island

North Carolina and Rhode Island were the two states that actually rejected the Constitution — at first.

Nine days after New York ratified, the North Carolina convention defeated ratification by a whopping 184-84. It stayed out of the new union for more than a year before finally ratifying 194-77 at a second convention in November of 1789, after the Bill of Rights had been approved by the first Congress and referred to the states.

Rhode Island, the smallest state, the first to make the break with England in 1775, had been a nuisance to the federalists from the beginning. It was the only state that refused to send a delegation to the Philadelphia convention. Then it was the only state that refused to call a ratifying convention to consider the new Constitution. Instead, the Legislature just asked the citizens for a direct up-or-down vote on the Constitution.

The proposed Supreme Law of the Land failed: 2,708 opposed to 237 in favor.

Into 1790, after Washington had been elected president and taken office, Rhode Island clung to its lonely position that the rest of the country had, in essence, seceded from *it*.

In 1790, Rhode Island finally called a ratifying convention, which approved the Constitution by a whopping margin of 34 in favor, 32 opposed.

E Pluribus Unum.

8

Slavery Versus
the Blessings of Liberty

In 1861 Congress passed and referred to the states an amendment to the U.S. Constitution guaranteeing that Congress could never abolish slavery.

Abraham Lincoln, elected but not yet inaugurated, endorsed it.

It was only an explicit restatement of a principle already firmly fixed in the Constitution, he said, so "I have no objection to its being made express and irrevocable." The amendment was not ratified.

The anecdote strikes harshly against our image of Lincoln the friend of the slaves, the Great Emancipator.

But it is consistent with Lincoln's position until well into the Civil War. He believed that slavery was immoral, but constitutionally protected. He did not seek its abolition.

Furthermore, Lincoln was correct. Slavery was constitutional as all get out. The Constitution we think of as the guarantor of rights and freedoms was written by slaveholders and was the guarantor of their right to deprive others of their freedom.

We don't want it to be true. We scour the records for evidence that will enable us to deny it. Surely the Founding Fathers, whose preamble says the Constitution was established to "secure the blessings of liberty for ourselves and our posterity," must have intended those blessings for all Americans. But no amount of scouring can remove the stain.

The Framers on Slavery

The members of the Constitutional Convention didn't invent slavery, nor did they legalize it. But they did more than neutrally condone the institution. They rewarded slave states, granting them extra representation in Congress, and they strengthened slavery, making it unconstitutional for a free state to harbor a fugitive slave.

The Constitution prohibited Congress from outlawing the slave trade for 20 years after the charter was ratified. And it enabled Congress to tax the importation of new slaves, but not more than $10 a head. The year and dollar amount were written into the document, although the framers went to some lengths to keep the word "slave" out.

And, as Lincoln said 74 years later, Congress lacked the power to abolish slavery. In fact, even though a number of the Northern delegates disliked slavery, no one at the convention suggested that Congress be empowered to abolish it.

Slavery was denounced a few times at the convention, but the legal status of human bondage took no damage.

Delegate George Mason said: "Every master of slaves is born a petty tyrant; they bring the judgment of heaven on a country."

That Mason was a rich Virginia planter makes his position appear all the more noble — at first glance. The second glance is a bit disheartening. He didn't suggest that slavery be outlawed by the Constitution, nor even that Congress be empowered to end the institution eventually. In fact, Mason owned 200 slaves himself, and he later complained that the Constitution didn't provide *enough* safeguards for slaveowners' rights.

Mason made that anti-slavery remark because he wanted to end the importation of new slaves from Africa. But even here his motives are suspect. Virginia already had a large, self-sustaining slave population. It didn't need the slave trade.

South Carolina and Georgia, less-developed states in which the warmer climate and more strenuous agricultural practices tended to lower the life expectancy of slaves, sought an influx of new ones. If slaves couldn't be captured from Africa, Georgia and South Carolina planters would have to buy them from Virginia.

Gouverneur Morris of Pennsylvania, the peg-legged draftsman of the Constitution, called slavery a "nefarious institution, the curse of heaven on the states where it prevails."

But neither Morris nor Ben Franklin (who was president of the Philadelphia Anti-slavery Society) nor anyone else suggested that the Constitution should abolish slavery. To do so would have ended the possibility of union.

Consulting Their Interests

Delegate John Rutledge of South Carolina laid it on the line thusly: "Religion and humanity has nothing to do with this question ... The true question at present is whether the Southern States shall or shall not be parties to the Union. If the Northern States consult their interests, they will not oppose the increase of slaves which will increase the commodities of which they will become the carriers." (Northern shipping interests carried the cotton, rice and tobacco produced by Southern slaves for sale overseas.)

New England delegates did "consult their interests" and supported the continuation of the slave trade in exchange for Southern concessions on navigation laws.

How would slaves count in the calculation of a state's population for voting power in the House of Representatives?

The slave-state delegates wanted full credit, which would have given them dominance in the House. The Northerners wanted no credit given, which would have given them dominance.

Virginian James Madison, father of the Constitution, himself a slaveholder but one who had moral qualms about the institution, favored full counting of slaves.

Elbridge Gerry of Massachusetts said that if the Southern farmers could get representation for their property (slaves), Northerners should get representation for their horses and cattle.

Gouverneur Morris argued: "The admission of slaves into the representation comes to this: that the inhabitant of Georgia and South Carolina who goes to the coast of Africa and, in defiance of the most sacred laws of humanity, tears away his fellow creatures from their dearest connections and damns them to the most cruel bondage, shall have more votes in a government instituted for protection of the rights of mankind than the citizen of Pennsylvania or New Jersey, who views with a laudable horror so nefarious a practice."

This is indeed what happened under the compromise that was adopted. A slave would be counted as three-fifths of a person. The impact of the slave population on the census was that five voters in a slave state had representation in the House equal to seven voters in a non-slave state.

Slavery was an issue at some of the ratifying conventions. One delegate to the Massachusetts convention in 1788 attacked slaveholder George Washington, who had presided over the Constitutional Convention and would soon preside over a lot more:

"O! Washington, what a name he has had. How he has immortalized himself. But he holds those in slavery who have as good a right to be free as he has. He is still for self and in my opinion his character has sunk fifty percent."

The Civil War

Slavery haunted the Constitution like an original sin. It would drag constitutional history through some of its ugliest moments and would precipitate the Constitution's biggest crisis — the Civil War.

When we think about the events leading to the Civil War, many tend to think the argument was between those who wanted to abolish slavery and those who wanted it maintained. Not so.

Certainly there was an abolitionist movement. In 1843 William Lloyd Garrison, the abolitionist leader, called the Constitution "a covenant with death and an agreement with hell!" He advocated secession by the Northern states to free them from association with slave states.

On the Fourth of July in 1854 he publicly burned a copy of the Constitution, saying, "So perish all compromises with tyranny." Even among abolitionists, this was viewed as a tad on the strong side. Other abolitionists favored working within a constitutional framework.

But abolitionists were a small faction. No law to abolish slavery ever got anywhere in Congress before the Civil War, nor did any major party ever nominate for president anyone who advocated abolition.

Instead, the argument was over slavery in the Western territories and its status as those territories became states.

Lincoln's position as he came to national prominence in 1858 was opposed to extending slavery into new states. He hoped it would gradually die out, and favored recolonization of freed slaves in Africa.

When the Civil War broke out, Lincoln maintained he couldn't free the slaves. When Union commanders issued orders freeing slaves in captured territories, Lincoln disavowed the orders.

So how did Lincoln square his belief in the constitutionality of slaveowners' rights with his eventual Emancipation Proclamation of 1863?

He justified it as an emergency military action, and limited its application to slaves in the seceded states. Slavery remained legal in the border states that had not seceded. In other words, it applied only to areas over which the federal government had no control, and didn't actually free any slaves at the time.

In 1865, 78 years after the drafting of the Constitution, the 13th Amendment abolished slavery. The 14th Amendment in 1868 granted citizenship, due-process rights and equal protection to the freed slaves.

That amendment, and the legal status of freed slaves and their descendants, have been a major focus of constitutional history ever since.

A SHORT CONSTITUTIONAL

In the Dred Scott decision of 1857, slavery and the Supreme Court dragged the U.S. Constitution to one of its all-time lows of immorality and inequality.

Dred Scott was a slave, owned by a military surgeon. In 1833 Scott's master took him from the slave state of Missouri to the free state of Illinois. In 1836 they moved to Fort Snelling in the federal territory near what would become the city of St. Paul, Minn. Congress had banned slavery in the Northern portions of the federal territory.

Scott lived at Fort Snelling much of the next four years, during which he married Harriet, the slave of another military officer.

In 1846, after the Scotts had been brought back to Missouri, they sued for their freedom, arguing that they had been permanently freed by living so long on free soil.

It took 11 years for the case to reach the U.S. Supreme Court. When the court finally handed down its decision, it was a doozy.

The court ruled against the Scotts, 7-2. But the decision went a lot further than keeping one family in bondage.

It ruled that no black person — free or slave — was or could ever be a U.S. citizen.

When the Constitution was adopted, Chief Justice Roger Taney wrote, blacks were "so far inferior" to whites "that they had no rights which the white man was bound to respect; and ... might justly and lawfully be reduced to slavery for their benefit."

Taney, a Maryland native whose political sympathies were

with slave owners, also ruled that Congress lacked constitutional power to prohibit slavery in the territories. The decision upset the fragile balance that had enabled the slave and free states to avoid open conflict. The Dred Scott decision is often cited as one of the contributing causes of the Civil War.

Abolitionists attacked the decision. The New York Tribune said the Supreme Court's decision had "just so much moral weight as . . . the judgment of a majority of those congregated in any Washington barroom."

Woman suffrage leader Susan B. Anthony, also active in the abolition cause, said that unfortunately "Taney's decision, infamous as it is, is but the reflection of the spirit and practice of the American people, North as well as South."

The Scotts were freed soon after the decision by the man who had become their master. They remained in St. Louis, where Dred worked as a hotel porter and Harriet as a laundress.

9

Democracy and the Framers

The U.S. Constitution did not establish democracy in America.

In fact, democracy may have declined when the Constitution became the law of the land in 1788.

Blasphemy? Yes, but . . .

The Constitution, when it took effect, did not give the vote to anyone who didn't already have it — specifically white, male, adult property owners composing roughly 15 percent of the population.

Nor did it increase popular control over government. Instead it created one body — the House of Representatives — that was directly responsible to the voters, and three others — the Senate, the presidency and the Supreme Court — to be chosen by a variety of indirect methods.

"None of the (state) constitutions have provided sufficient checks against democracy," Virginia's Edmund Randolph said on the opening day of the Constitutional Convention in 1787.

"The evils we experience flow from the excess of democracy," said Massachusetts delegate Elbridge Gerry a week later.

Madison referred to the "inconvenience of democracy," Hamilton to the "imprudence" of it. Rather than isolated remarks, these were the mainstream sentiments of the convention.

Bear in mind, democracy was not the sacred principle it is now. It was experimental, scary and based on the belief — not inherently appealing to an elite group — that men of less property, less learning, less breeding should be allowed to govern themselves.

State of the art democratic theory at the time held that a republic was most democratic when it was small, simple and direct. The framers designed one that was large, complex and indirect.

The Constitution was, in short, an elitist document, written by members of an elite class and designed to increase the chances that members of that class would remain in control.

In the 200 years since, the democratic content of the Constitution has increased. But some of the anti-democratic odor put on the system by the framers still clings.

To be sure, the United States in 1787 was a shining beacon of democracy compared to the rest of the world, where hereditary monarchies prevailed.

The American experiment in government by consent of the governed was a turning point in world history. The American and French revolutions of the 1770's and '80's started a democratic trend that has never stopped. Before those revolutions, the divine right of kings was the basis of governmental power. Two centuries later, even the most despotic rulers feel obliged to make some pretense of possessing a popular mandate.

But America's great contribution to that trend was made 11 years before the framers of the Constitution did their framing.

The Spirit of '76

The Declaration of Independence staked out the high ground in 1776. That document asserted the self-evident truth that all men have equal, God-given rights to life, liberty and the pursuit of happiness.

The purpose of government is to secure those rights, the Declaration argued, and a just government must derive its powers from the consent of the governed.

The spirit of '76 was reflected in the Pennsylvania constitution written at that time. That document was so radically democratic that even officers of the state militia were elected.

By 1787, the framers had seen democracy at work on the state level, and they didn't like what they saw. As Madison put it, the period had been characterized by "local mischiefs which everywhere excite disgust."

In fact, one can view the Constitution as essentially a conservative counter-revolution in which the elite reasserted their authority over the masses, who were getting a bit uppity.

The U.S. Constitution did not repeal the state charters, of course, but it was supreme over them and it lacked their most democratic aspects.

The system with which the framers were most familiar was England's, where the power of the people, reflected in the House of Commons, was balanced by the aristocracy (in the House of Lords) and ultimate authority still belonged to the king.

But America had no king and no hereditary ruling class. The convention delegates themselves had been appointed by the elected state legislatures. And nothing written at the convention would matter unless ratified by a public that was enthralled with this new concept of democracy.

So if, as the counter-revolution theory suggests, the framers wanted to reduce the democratic content of the system, they didn't have much to work with.

What's a founding father to do?

Indirectness

One approach was to put filters between the common people and the choice of federal officials. "The people immediately should have as little to do as may be about the government," was the way Connecticut delegate Roger Sherman put it.

The selection of senators would be filtered through the state legislatures, the selection of the president filtered through the Electoral College and the selection of the Supreme Court justices through the president and the senators who had already been filtered.

The House of Representatives would be elected directly. This was to be the democratic element of the system. It won easy acceptance at the convention, although South Carolina delegate Charles Pinckney protested in a later letter to Madison:

"Are you not ... abundantly impressed that the theoretical nonsense of an election of Congress by the people in the first instance is clearly and practically wrong, that it will in the end be the means of bringing our councils into contempt?"

The question of who would get to vote in these elections was more difficult. Franchise requirements varied from state to state. The most liberal was Pennsylvania, where white male taxpayers could vote. In most states a certain amount of property or wealth was necessary. In New York a complicated system required one level of wealth to vote for the lower house of the state legislature and still more wealth to vote for state senators. The framers decided to let state requirements stand. If you couldn't vote for a state representative, you couldn't vote for a congressman either.

Complexity

Pennsylvania's state-of-the-art democratic constitution of 1776 set up a one-house legislature, elected annually, with weak executive and judicial branches. The idea was simple: You had one representative to your government, you would pick him once a year and give him a clear idea of what you wanted in the way of government that year. Politicians who strayed would soon be back to face the people; those who didn't stray would be back for fresh instructions.

In the constitutional system, simplicity is replaced with complexity. Every two years, a House member gets elected. Every four years, a president is chosen; every six years, a senator. For the electorate's wishes to become law, they have to be passed by both houses and signed by the president (or a veto overridden by two-thirds of each house) and be viewed as constitutional by a majority of the Supreme Court (although it is not clear that the framers intended this last hurdle).

Madison argued such complexities would provide checks and balances against half-baked ideas that might bubble up from the masses. To proponents of democracy, checks and balances was a fancy name for barriers to majority rule.

Largeness

A large republic was viewed as less democratic and more elitist, which from Madison's point of view was a great selling point. It showed the way to taming democracy without abolishing it.

"The only defense against the inconvenience of democracy consistent with the democratic form of government," Madison wrote, was "enlarging the sphere."

In one of the most famous of the Federalist Papers, Madison described the dangers of a small republic and the advantages of a larger one.

In a small republic, a majority could be dangerously homogenous. Its members could perceive themselves as all having the same problem, which they could solve at the expense of a minority. In such a situation, Madison feared that majority rule might overwhelm minority rights.

When we hear about minority rights nowadays, we first think of a racial or religious minority, or perhaps the minority that holds an unpopular political viewpoint or practices a minority life style.

Madison was not unsympathetic to some of these minorities. He was a strong defender of religious minorities. In some references, Madison even expressed sympathy for the slave minority, although such sympathy didn't prevent Madison from owning slaves.

But in the examples he uses, Madison makes clear that the

minority whose protection he has uppermost in mind is the minority of wealthy creditors. And the group threatening a tyranny of the majority is the majority of poor debtors.

In Rhode Island, representatives of the debtor class had used their superior numbers to issue paper money and run the state government so much for the benefit of the debtors that many rich creditors had fled the state. In Massachusetts, the dispute between the two classes had come to blows.

These were the kinds of "local mischiefs" Madison felt could be prevented by a larger republic, let us say one comprising 13 states.

A majority would have to be a coalition of groups from each of the states. Its membership would be less homogenous, less united, less clear in its goals and less able to extract a solution from the purses of the wealthy.

". . . A rage for paper money, for an abolition of debts, for an equal division of property, or for any other improper or wicked project, will be less apt to pervade the whole body of the Union than a particular member (state)," Madison wrote.

The framers' indirectness principle has been diluted by constitutional amendments and other changes. The right to vote has been extended several-fold. The complexity principle remains about the same and continues to be a target of complaints by those who feel our legislative system is too unwieldy.

But after 200 years the largeness principle may be more effective in protecting the interests of the wealthy than Madison ever dreamed.

In 1787, the framers pegged the size of the original congressional districts at 30,000 people. The public wouldn't buy any bigger districts than that, they felt.

Nowadays, congressional districts average 17 times that big, or 527,000 people. A U.S. senator from California has 27 million constituents.

The best way of relating contemporary elitism to the largeness principle is through campaign contributions.

A person running for a seat in Congress can't campaign through personal appearances, door knocking, neighborhood coffee parties, or phone banks operated by small committees of volunteers. A modern campaign for Congress requires billboards, newspaper and television advertising, media consultants. In short, you need big bucks. You either have that money yourself, in which case you are a member of the economic elite, or you make your peace with people who can provide you with that kind of money.

A SHORT CONSTITUTIONAL

The democratic content of the constitutional system has increased steadily over 200 years. Some highlights of the changes:

In the 1820's and 1830's, most states extended suffrage to white men, even if they lacked property. The changes were made through state constitutions.

In 1865, slavery was abolished (13th Amendment). In 1868, citizenship was extended to blacks (14th Amendment). In 1870, voting rights were guaranteed to black men (15th Amendment), although these rights were unenforced in some states until the 1960's and '70's.

In 1913, the Senate was made a directly elected body (17th Amendment).

In 1920, women gained voting rights (19th Amendment).

In 1964, poll taxes, which had been used to deny the vote to blacks, were written out of the Constitution (24th Amendment).

Also in 1964, the U.S. Supreme Court interpreted the concept of "one man, one vote" into the Constitution.

In 1971, 18- to 21-year-olds gained voting rights (26th Amendment).

Thanks to these changes, the proportion of Americans eligible to vote is at an all-time high of 75 percent (compared with an estimated 15 percent eligible when the nation was founded). Paradoxically, voter participation in 1986 was at a 40-year low of 37.3 percent of those eligible.

10

Matriculating at the Electoral College

Does the majority rule around here or what?

Not exactly. In the 1988 presidential election, for example, the winner might receive fewer votes than the loser.

That's not a prediction, but it has happened three times, and the possibility that it will happen again exists as long as the Electoral College system remains our way of choosing a chief executive.

The college is a vestige of the anti-democratic intentions of the framers of the U.S. Constitution, but the system doesn't function anything like the framers intended.

They didn't foresee party primaries, nor even political parties. Most surprising, they did not require that any popular vote be held for president. The Constitution still doesn't require it.

If a state passed a law canceling the popular election for president in 1988 and adopting some other method of selecting the state's presidential electors, it would be constitutional.

In the early years, some state legislatures didn't bother consulting the voters about who should be president. 1872 was the first presidential election in which all states held popular elections.

Presidents Jimmy Carter and Richard Nixon advocated abolishing the Electoral College system, but the Senate blocked the idea both times.

Thanks to the system, three men have been elected president who actually lost the popular vote (including one who also lost the electoral vote), two presidential elections have been determined in the House of Representatives, one presidential election was stolen and 15 presidents have been elected with less than a majority of the popular vote.

The lowest percentage of popular vote to translate into an electoral majority was in 1860, when Abraham Lincoln won with less than 40 percent of the votes cast in a four-way race.

Most of us learned the basics of the Electoral College in civics class. Each state has electoral votes equal to its number of U.S. representatives and senators. The winner of the popular vote in each state gets all of that state's electoral votes. The winner of a majority of electoral votes becomes president.

Those who stay up late on election night to watch the returns get a quadrennial refresher course in the Electoral College during one of the slow spots in the broadcast.

But neither the civics teacher — at least my civics teacher — nor the anchorman tell us *why* we have this system. Why not just let the one who gets the most votes be president?

Framing the Electoral College

The answer is that the framers of the Constitution did not trust the people to elect the president directly. They created the positions of presidential electors, who they expected would be members of the educated elite and who would stand between the ill-informed, easily inflamed public and the choice of a president.

As the Constitution set up the system, the voters would elect their state legislature and the legislature would select a delegation of leading citizens as electors. The electors of each state would meet (but not with the electors from other states) and vote.

If a legislature wanted to conduct a popular election, that was the legislature's business. But the Constitution didn't require it. South Carolina, one of the original states, didn't hold a popular presidential election until after the Civil War.

Who Elected Washington?

George Washington, the most famous, most admired American of his time, was the consensus choice to be the first president. The mechanics of his election in 1789, the first under the Constitution, show the options under the Electoral College system.

Four states held direct popular elections to choose electors. Four legislatures kept matters in their own hands. The New York Legislature intended to do that, but the two houses couldn't agree on how to pick electors and they discussed it until it was too late to participate.

Two states created a hybrid system in which the people voted but the legislature retained the real power.

North Carolina and Rhode Island hadn't ratified the Constitution in time and so didn't participate.

Washington remains the only president elected unanimously by the Electoral College. He did it in 1789 and 1792.

Deadlock Provisions

The Constitution also provides that if the Electoral College doesn't produce a majority, the president is chosen by the House of Representatives, with each state's House delegation casting one vote. (This is one of the less-famous concessions the framers made to the small states. Under this provision, Alaska's one House member, representing 500,000 Americans, would have a voice in the election of the president equal to the combined voice of the 45 congressmen who represent 27 million Californians.)

Several members of the 1787 Constitutional Convention believed that after Washington's election, the Electoral College was unlikely to produce majorities. They didn't foresee the rise of the party system, and imagined that the electors would scatter their votes.

In fact, only two elections have been decided in the House: Thomas Jefferson over Aaron Burr in 1800 (which is discussed on page 57) and John Quincy Adams over Andrew Jackson in 1824. There have been other close calls. Most recently, if Hubert Humphrey had carried California in 1968 (he didn't miss by that much), the Humphrey-Richard Nixon-George Wallace election would have been thrown into the House.

The "Corrupt Bargain" of 1824

As late as 1820, the 10th presidential election, nine of the 24 states still sent a delegation to the Electoral College without giving the public a chance to vote for president.

Popular votes for president became widespread in the 1824 election, when 18 of the 24 states chose their electors by popular vote.

Ironically, that first "popular" election had a very unpopular outcome because, for the only time in U.S. history, it resulted in the election of a president who had won neither the popular nor electoral vote.

In a four-man field, Andrew Jackson, hero of the War of 1812, received the most popular and electoral votes, but not a majority. The House ended up electing second-place finisher John Quincy

Adams. Fourth-place finisher Henry Clay had given Adams a key endorsement. So when Adams appointed Clay secretary of state, the Jacksonians insisted that the two had engaged in a "corrupt bargain." The issue stigmatized the Adams administration. Jackson whomped Adams in an 1828 rematch.

Triple Teaming Van Buren

In 1836, the Whig Party ran three men for president, each in the region where the candidate was strongest. The idea was to elect a majority of electors who could combine to produce an electoral victory for a Whig. But Democratic candidate Martin Van Buren, running all by his lonesome, captured a popular and electoral majority.

In 1876, Democrat Samuel Tilden beat Republican Rutherford B. Hayes in popular vote and should have won an electoral majority as well. Republicans used their control of the state governments and the election machinery in conquered Southern states to claim fraudulently the electoral votes of South Carolina, Florida and Louisiana. If they could make those claims stand, Hayes would win by one electoral vote.

The dispute became so tense that a renewal of the Civil War seemed threatened.

Congress created a special commission of 15 senators, congressmen and Supreme Court justices to decide the election dispute. The party makeup of the commission was eight Republicans and seven Democrats. And sure enough, by a series of 8-7 votes, the commission adopted the Republican arguments and stole the election for Hayes.

In 1888, Republican Benjamin Harrison lost the popular vote but won the electoral vote and became president, the third and last time that that has happened.

Members of the Electoral College are legally free to vote for whomever they think will make the best president. In current practice, the electors are generally committed to vote for the nominee of their party, but in six of the last 10 elections one elector has broken that commitment.

A SHORT CONSTITUTIONAL

A little glitch in this country's Electoral College system almost cost the young republic the services of one of its greatest presidents in the hotly contested election of 1800.

The U.S. Constitution originally called for each elector to vote for two people. The person who received the most votes would be president, the runner-up would be vice president. The president and vice president might be one another's worst political enemies, as happened during the presidency of John Adams (1797-1801) when his prime political opponent, Thomas Jefferson, was vice president.

By the election of 1800, the first version of the two-party system had developed. Jefferson led his party, the Democratic Republicans, to electoral victory over Adams' Federalists. The Democratic Republican electors each cast one vote for Jefferson and one for his running mate, Aaron Burr of New York.

But the Constitution didn't allow them to designate one vote for president and the other for vice president (remember, the vice president was supposed to be the runner-up). The result was the first and only electoral tie, throwing the election into the House of Representatives.

This was not just a technicality, because the House was still controlled by the Federalists. Burr probably could have been elected president if he had made enough political deals with Federalist congressmen. Or he might have averted the crisis if he had acknowledged what everyone knew to be the case — that the electors had intended Jefferson to be president. He did neither.

Most, but not enough, Federalists supported Burr anyway because they hated Jefferson.

Alexander Hamilton, an influential Federalist, wrote: "I trust the Federalists will not finally be so mad as to vote for Burr. I speak with intimate and accurate knowledge of his character. His elevation can only promote the purposes of the desperate and profligate. If there be a man in the world I ought to hate, it is Jefferson. With Burr I have always been personally well. But the public good must be paramount to every private consideration."

Hamilton and Burr belonged to opposing political factions in New York. In 1804 Burr killed Hamilton in a duel.

Jefferson wrote that he had been offered votes for future favors. "Many attempts have been made to obtain terms and promises from me. I have declared to them unequivocally that I would not receive the Government on capitulation; that I would not go in with my hands tied."

After 36 ballots, over the course of a week, Jefferson was elected president and Burr became vice president. Needless to say, Jefferson dumped Burr as his running mate for his sec-ond term, and later seized an opportunity to declare Burr a traitor. Burr was charged with treason but acquitted in 1807.

The electoral crisis of 1800 inspired Congress to pass (in 1803) and the states to ratify (in 1804) the 12th Amendment to the Constitution, enabling electors to designate which of their votes was for president.

11

1787 in Context

The year: 1787.

In Austria, Wolfgang Amadeus Mozart writes the opera "Don Giovanni." In Algiers, bubonic plague kills 17,000 people. In China, the island of Formosa rebels against the emperor. The empress of Russia and the Ottoman emperor go to war but, following tradition, they let their troops do the actual fighting and dying.

Capitalism is a new idea. The word hasn't even been coined. The industrial revolution is taking off in Europe and catching on in America, where the first American cotton mill opens in Massachusetts. Steamboats are a hot item; the first one in America chugs along the Delaware River in 1787. The properties and uses of electricity are explored. The western edge of the white man's control in America is Ohio.

And in Philadelphia in May, 55 framers-to-be of the U.S. Constitution hang up their tri-cornered hats and start to do some framing.

With the benefit of hindsight and from the world view of Americans, the Constitutional Convention eclipses other world events of the period. But at the time it would have been hard to say which contemporary happenings would be celebrated and studied 200 years later.

In looking at events outside of Philadelphia in 1787, the purpose is not to help answer trivia questions no one will ever ask. The purpose is to understand, in the context of its own time, the American Revolution, from the Declaration of Independence to the framing of the Constitution.

For example, events in London in 1788, where a weak king would become a crazy king, underscore the revolutionary nature of the new American system.

Events in Paris in 1789, where a king and great gaggles of the gentry were on their way to losing their heads, suggest the essential conservatism and remarkable stability of the American Revolution.

An event in New York in the summer of 1787, where the pre-Constitution Congress, still in business, enacted a progressive piece of landmark legislation, militates against the myth of the Constitution as America's engine of social progress.

Virtues of the No-king System

In London, George III, having lost his American colonies, also lost his mind (in 1788) but not his crown. George would live — and reign — for 32 more years, during which his sanity would come and go.

George, who was seldom mistaken for a great leader even when in his right mind, held the throne for 60 years (1760-1820), one of the longest reigns in English history. (Charles, the current Prince of Wales, who will reign himself someday, cites George III as his favorite king.)

George was not an evil tyrant, as he is sometimes conveniently portrayed in popular histories of the American Revolution. But he was a weak leader, trapped by royal birth in a role too big for his abilities.

The bout of insanity in 1788 was temporary, but he was fully and permanently crazy for the last nine years of his life, during which the prince of Wales acted as regent.

The royal insanity suggests at least one of the problems of monarchy as a system of government. There's no easy way to get rid of an insane king, let alone a bad or a weak or a power-hungry or war-mongering one. His term of office is for life, and he is not subject to impeachment.

By 1787, to be sure, several European nations had limited the power of their kings. Iceland had had a parliament, the Althing, since 930. (It still has it — the oldest continuous parliamentary body in existence.)

England under George had a powerful Parliament. His ministers constituted something like an executive branch. But it wasn't like today, where the royal role is largely ceremonial.

George III could fire a minister or defeat a bill. He single-mindedly blocked efforts to liberalize anti-Catholic laws.

In some countries, the era of liberalization was over. In Sweden, a period of experimentation with a limited monarchy was ended by Gustavus III, who restored absolute royal government by means of military coups in 1772 and 1789.

For all its defects, monarchy was the system in every European country in 1787. Every white settlement in the new world — except the United States — was owned by a European king.

Other countries had rebelled against the tyranny of a particular king or emperor. Others had asserted that a king had an obligation to serve the interests of his subjects. But the divine right of kings had been the basis of governmental authority in the Western world since the Roman Republic became the Roman Empire in the last century B.C.

Then these crazy Americans assert that divine rights are given to all men, and that kings are a convenience a nation may choose to live with or without.

The Constitution of 1787, of course, did not establish that principle. The Declaration of Independence did it in 1776. But in the 1780's, talk of a return to monarchy, either by adopting some European prince or by crowning George Washington, was heard.

For all their elitist tendencies, the framers expressly prohibited the U.S. government from granting any titles of nobility and forbade any government official from accepting a title from a foreign king. In short, the Constitution secured the "no-king" system, and in the context of 1787, that was a revolutionary doctrine.

Two Revolutions

France, the most powerful country in Europe at the time, was not one of the countries that had developed a strong parliament to balance the king. The Estates General, the closest thing France had to a parliament, hadn't met for more than 150 years when Louis XVI summoned it in May 1789.

Talk about opening a Pandora's box. By June the middle-class members of the assembly had asserted control over the king, the aristocracy and the clergy. In July a Paris mob stormed the Bastille, symbol of royal power, and in the countryside peasants burned the houses of their feudal lords. By year's end, Paris was governed by a commune, aristocrats fled in droves, the landed estates of the church had been nationalized and Louis XVI, while still wearing his head, had lost his power. (He and his wife, Marie Antoinette, would be guillotined in 1793.)

Over the next 10 years, France endured a breathtaking series of revolutions, followed by more radical revolutions, followed by counter-revolutions. The leaders of each phase were beheaded by the leaders of the next phase. Power generally traveled downward in the social hierarchy. The monarchy ceased to be, the aristocracy ceased to be, and middle-class leaders held power only with the support of mobs of urban poor.

One faction appealed to the masses in 1793 with a proposed "Constitution of the Year One," which called for the uncompensated confiscation of all remaining feudal lands and redistribution of the land on terms low enough for the poorest peasants to afford.

After 10 years of upheaval, the revolution culminated with Napoleon Bonaparte declaring himself emperor.

What does any of this have to do with the U.S. Constitution? It points by contrast to the conservatism and stability of the American system.

George Washington, Benjamin Franklin, John Adams and men of their class were the rulers of America before, during and after the American Revolution. Our revolution lacked the radical social and economic aspects of the French version. The 55 members of the Constitutional Convention were members of the social and economic elite, and the system they framed preserved the favored position of their class.

In France, guys like the framers got their heads chopped off. In America, we ratified the Constitution they wrote, then started electing them president.

Some members of America's pre-war ruling class, those Loyalists who clung to their king, had to leave. But many were paid for their property. The land was sold by the states to those who could afford it, not redistributed to the peasantry, as happened in France. Nothing in America resembled the Paris Commune of 1793 for radical experimentation.

But if America's revolution can't match France's for violent swings to the left, neither did it veer wildly to the right. America's counter-revolution was the adoption of the Constitution itself, a retrenchment of democracy and equality from the more revolutionary tone of the Declaration of Independence. After 10 years of upheaval, France ended up with an emperor.

Two hundred years after 1787, the United States finds itself possessor of the world's oldest working constitution. The 13 states have become 50. The population has increased seventyfold. We've been through five declared wars and countless other incursions and interventions. Our enemies have become our allies and our allies have become our enemies. The Constitution wrought that year in

Philadelphia has been amended 26 times and interpreted nine ways from Sunday. But it's still standing.

By contrast, France has been governed by two Bonapartist empires, two restorations of the Bourbon monarchy, a Nazi puppet regime and five different republican forms of government, the most recent adopted in 1958.

Engine of Social Progress

According to myth, the adoption of the U.S. Constitution was necessary because our previous government, under the Articles of Confederation, was inadequate. Another notion about the Constitution is that it has been a force for social progress. Under the principles and teachings of the Constitution, the United States has evolved into a land of freedom and equality, or so goes the myth.

So you may be surprised that the Confederation Congress, still in business in New York while the framers in Philadelphia drew up the terms of its demise, adopted a vigorous, wise and extraordinarily progressive law.

The Northwest Ordinance of 1787 provided for the governance of the area that would become Ohio, Indiana, Illinois, Michigan, Wisconsin and the part of Minnesota east of the Mississippi.

Up to five territories from that region could apply for statehood when their populations reached 60,000, the ordinance said. Each would be accepted "on an equal footing with the original states in all respects whatsoever."

In four very important areas, the ordinance was far more progressive than the Constitution.

■ Slavery: The Constitution condoned and strengthened slavery in the existing slave states. The ordinance prohibited slavery in the Northwest territories.

■ Civil liberties: Freedom of religion and the right to a jury trial were guaranteed in the territories by the Northwest Ordinance. The Constitution, before amendment, was silent on the subject.

■ Public education: The Constitution makes no mention of education, leaving it as a matter for the individual states. Some states, especially in New England, provided primary schooling at public expense. Southern states took little or no responsibility for educating poor children. In the middle states, elementary schools were generally parochial or philanthropic.

In the Northwest Ordinance, the national government guaranteed free public education and set aside one acre of every township for a school.

■ Indian rights: The Constitution mentions Indians twice, once to say they won't be counted toward a state's representation in Congress, and a second time empowering Congress to regulate commerce with the tribes.

The Northwest Ordinance, by contrast, contains a grand statement of good intentions. It reads: "The utmost good faith shall always be observed toward the Indians, their lands and property shall never be taken from them without their consent; and in their property, rights and liberty, they shall never be invaded or disturbed unless in just and lawful wars authorized by Congress; but laws founded in justice and humanity shall from time to time be made, for preventing wrongs being done to them, and for preserving peace and friendship with them."

Many of these good intentions were violated, as were a series of treaties between the Congress and tribal governments. But you have to wonder whether the rights, liberty and property of the tribes might have been better respected if such a pledge had been in the Constitution itself, instead of being contained in a statute passed by a Congress that was itself on the edge of extinction.

12

Marbury, Madison and Marshall

If you want to get a law professor misted up about the U.S. Constitution, mention the case of Marbury vs. Madison.

That's the case lawyers study first when they learn constitutional law. It's the fountain from which the rest of constitutional law flows.

In its ruling on that case, the U.S. Supreme Court in 1803 first exercised its power to declare acts of Congress unconstitutional. But more than just using the power, the court, in a way, *invented* that power, which the Constitution does not clearly give to the court.

Alexander Bickel, a renowned modern constitutional scholar, said of the Marbury decision: "It is hallowed, it is revered. If it had a physical presence, like the Alamo or Gettysburg, it would be a tourist attraction."

Chief Justice John Marshall (1755-1835) owes a goodly chunk of his heroic historical reputation to his authorship of the Marbury decision, which is usually portrayed as courageous, statesmanlike, highly judicious and — assuming that one believes the power of the Supreme Court to have been a positive force in constitutional history — a jolly good thing.

What the law professors may not tell their students is that the background of the Marbury case itself, and especially Marshall's role, is covered with hardball politics, nepotism, opportunism, expediency and gigantic conflicts of interest.

In fact, the law Marshall struck down in his decision was most likely constitutional. The decision was more clever than courageous, more a triumph of partisanship than statesmanship.

Here's the background of the case.

"Midnight Judges"

A new democracy faces one of its biggest tests when the party in office loses an election. Do they peacefully yield power or, as has happened in many countries, do they declare an emergency, suspend the constitution and keep counting the ballots till it comes out right?

The first test of the American system occurred in 1800 when Thomas Jefferson, leader of the Democratic Republicans, beat the incumbent Federalist President John Adams.

Adams didn't suspend the Constitution, but he didn't exactly leave office graciously. For example, he was one of only two presidents who refused to attend the inauguration of his successor. (The other one was Adams' son, John Quincy Adams, in 1829.

That was only a symbolic snub. But how's this for gracelessness of a lame duck: During January and February of 1801, after the election but before the inauguration, the Federalist majority in Congress:

■ Confirmed John Marshall, Adams' highly political secretary of state, as chief justice, so Jefferson couldn't appoint a chief justice. (Marshall ended up holding office until 1835, long after the Federalists had evaporated as a national party.)

■ Reduced the Supreme Court from six justices to five (so Jefferson would be deprived of his first Supreme Court appointment).

■ Created 19 federal judgeships and 53 other judicial and legal positions so Adams could load up the judicial branch with dozens of Federalists who would hold office for life.

Adams and Marshall (in those days, the secretary of state handled the paperwork on judicial appointments) had about a week to process the appointment of their friends and relatives to all those vacancies.

Marshall's brother got a judgeship for the District of Columbia and two of his brothers-in-law got circuit judgeships, as did President Adams' son-in-law. In their haste and determination to fill the positions with members of their party, Adams and Marshall overlooked small blots on the records of some of their appointees, like the one who had led English loyalist troops in the fight against American independence.

In the days before word processing, cranking out this many appointments in a week was a grueling task. Secretary of State Marshall (and bear in mind he was already sworn in as chief justice at the time) appointed judges until about 9 p.m. on the last night of the Adams presidency. Historians have dubbed the appointees "midnight judges," because that sounded snazzier than "9 p.m. judges."

A Bungled Commission

Among the positions created were 42 justice of the peaceships for the District of Columbia, which had become the capital in 1800. Among the Federalists who were supposed to get those jobs was William Marbury. In the chaos of the last day of the Adams administration, a few commissions were signed and sealed but not delivered. Marbury's commission was one.

When Jefferson took office the next day, he was faced with a judiciary that might as well have been named the Federalist Party branch of government.

Jefferson wrote to a friend that the Federalists had "retired into the judiciary as a stronghold."

"There the remains of federalism are to be preserved & fed from the treasury, and from that battery all the works of republicanism are to be beaten down and erased by a fraudulent use of the constitution which has made judges irremovable, they have multiplied useless judges merely to strengthen their phalanx," Jefferson wrote.

Jefferson refused to add to his problem by delivering Marbury's commission. In fact, the commission apparently was thrown out with the first load of Jeffersonian trash.

Jefferson also steered a bill through Congress in 1802 that repealed the act that created all the midnight judgeships. Many of Adams' top judicial appointees (not Marshall) were unappointed.

Now if you wanted to have a constitutional confrontation, this would make a grand issue to have it over. The Constitution says federal judges enjoy lifetime tenure. The midnight judge law, while politically nasty, was a bona fide act of Congress. And here are the executive and legislative branches ganging up to fire most of the members of the federal judiciary from their lifetime appointments.

If you want to strike something down, one wants to say to Marshall, forget Marbury and his stupid little justice of the peaceship. Strike down this repeal law, which is truly an assault on the separation of powers.

That might have been courageous, but also dumb. Jefferson and the Republican Congress would have flouted the court's action, refused to pay the judges' salaries and ignored any judgments they might render.

The precedent established would be that a court decision was not binding on the other branches, the opposite of what Marshall was trying to prove. So the Federalist Supreme Court took a dive, and allowed the repeal to stand.

But the law creating Marbury's justice of the peaceship wasn't repealed. Marbury sued, asking the court to order James Madison (Jefferson's secretary of state) to fork over his commission.

The Supreme Court, with Marshall presiding, actually held the trial. Madison, the defendant, ignored it. The Jefferson administration showed its contempt by offering no defense. Marbury's lawyer had to prove that Marbury had been appointed properly and only the delivery of the commission had been bungled without mentioning that the bungler was the man now presiding over the trial.

Thus, the most famous decision by the most illustrious chief justice came in a case in which he had a colossal conflict of interests. Under the ethical standards of today, he would have to disqualify himself from the case.

Consider Marshall's dilemma. If he decided in favor of Marbury, Jefferson could ignore the ruling, thus setting the wrong precedent from Marshall's point of view. But if Marshall ruled against Marbury, it would amount to another dive and another Jeffersonian victory over the Federalists. Here's how Marshall ruled:

Jefferson was wrong and Marbury was right on the merits. Marbury *should* get his justice of the peaceship. But Jefferson wins anyway because the Supreme Court doesn't have the power to order Jefferson to give Marbury the job, nor even the power to hold the trial in this case.

True, there was a law on the books that *appeared* to give the court jurisdiction over this case, but it is unconstitutional because the law gives the court more power than the Constitution gives it.

Now consider the tactical brilliance of the decision.

■ Marshall gets to lecture Jefferson for refusing to honor Marbury's appointment. That draws applause from the Jefferson-hating Federalists.

■ The court doesn't appear to be grabbing power, because the law Marshall strikes down is one that actually *gives* a small power to the court.

■ But in giving away that small power, Marshall claims for the court a new power a thousand times greater — the power to overrule Congress and give the final, binding interpretation of the Constitution.

■ Jefferson can't defy the court by rejecting the outcome because Jefferson wins the case.

What's Unconstitutional?

Brilliant yes, but was it legally sound? Just what was so unconstitutional about the law Marshall struck down?

The answer is probably nothing. Here's how Marshall claimed the law was unconstitutional:

Under the Constitution, the basic job of the Supreme Court is to decide appeals from trials held in lower courts. But the Supreme Court can hold the actual trials in a few small categories of cases such as those involving ambassadors, the Constitution says.

The Judiciary Act of 1789 said the Supreme Court could hold the original trials in a few *other* categories of cases, including those in which a plaintiff asks the court to order a federal official to do something. Since Marbury was asking the court to order Jefferson and Madison to do something (hand over his commission), his case came under the Judiciary Act duties of the court.

Marshall's decision said the Judiciary Act couldn't authorize the court to issue the order Marbury wanted, because the law gave the court powers beyond those mentioned in the Constitution. The Constitution does say that Congress can make exceptions and regulations to the Supreme Court's duties, but Marshall ignored that language. To do otherwise would have plunged him back into his dilemma.

In posing as the protector of the framers' intent, Marshall was taking on the framers themselves. The act Marshall struck down had been co-authored by Sen. Oliver Ellsworth, an influential member of the Constitutional Convention who left the Senate in 1796 to become chief justice. (His retirement in 1800 created the vacancy Marshall filled.)

Sitting on the bench next to Marshall as he struck down the law was Associate Justice William Paterson of New Jersey. Also a veteran of the constitutional convention, Paterson had considered the law constitutional enough to support it as a member of the first Senate, but in 1803 he went along with striking it down.

In fact, the Congress that passed the law included 13 members of the constitutional convention, all of whom appear to have supported the bill and none of whom suggested that anything in the law conflicted with the Constitution they had written two years earlier.

And finally, the law was signed by President George Washington, who had also been president of the Constitutional Convention.

So here's Marshall saying that these men who wrote the

Constitution and also wrote or supported the Judiciary Act didn't realize that the act violated the Constitution. But that he, who was not a member of the Constitutional Convention, must preserve the work of the framers by striking down a law the framers had written.

More than 50 years went by before the court stuck down another federal law. Marshall, Jefferson, Madison and Marbury were in their graves by then and the power of judicial review had somehow, without being exercised, become an unassailable, if unwritten, section of the myth that binds us.

The power has been exercised more than 100 times since then. In a unanimous 1958 decision, the court attributed much of its (by then) enormous power to the precedent established in Marbury. That case "declared the basic principle that the federal judiciary is supreme in the exposition of the law of the Constitution, and that principle has ever since been respected by the Court and the Country as a permanent and indispensable feature of our constitutional system. It follows that the interpretation . . . enunciated by this Court . . . is the supreme law of the land."

Part Two:
THE BILL OF RIGHTS

13

The Framers Against the Bill of Rights

You can stand on a street corner in Washington, D.C., call Ronald Reagan a senile old warmonger and urge his impeachment. You can publish a newspaper right here in River City accusing the governor of advocating socialism, or you can advocate it yourself.

Why? The U.S. Constitution guarantees that you can. In fact, our Constitution is so committed to freedom of expression that it guarantees your right to badmouth the Constitution.

You can worship your God or your great-aunt or nobody at all. If you're charged with a crime, you're entitled to a lawyer, to confront your accusers at a speedy public jury trial with process that's due, protection that's equal, and you can neither be forced to incriminate yourself nor be tried twice for the same crime.

Why? Hey, this is America. We have rights — constitutional rights, by golly.

When we think about the Constitution, the idea of rights is never far behind, especially the rights guaranteed by the first 10 amendments, sometimes called the Bill of Rights, probably the most beloved part of the Constitution.

And when we think of the Constitution, another thought buzzing around our brains somewhere is of the framers, the 55 wig-wearing demigods who wrote our basic national charter at the Constitutional Convention in 1787.

But this is one of those cases where two plus two doesn't equal four. That is, the framers wrote the Constitution, and the Bill of Rights is part of the Constitution, but the framers didn't write the Bill of Rights. That's why the Bill of Rights is contained in amendments.

Okay, no big revelations so far. Perhaps a bit more surprising is that the framers overwhelmingly *rejected* the idea of a bill of rights and that most of them continued to argue after the convention that a written guarantee of rights was unnecessary and might do more harm than good.

The Declaration of Independence had said in 1776 that the purpose of government was to secure the inalienable rights of the people to life, liberty and the pursuit of happiness.

But the members of the Constitutional Convention of 1787 did not have rights so much on their minds as they worked through that hot summer in Philadelphia.

A few important rights were secured in the main body of the Constitution they drafted. But in the first 15 weeks of the 16-week convention, the idea of a general guarantee of rights was not raised, even though eight of the 13 states had such bills in their constitutions.

The new national charter was basically written and the convention was considering minor last-minute changes on Sept. 12, 1787, five days before adjournment, when delegate George Mason, himself the author of Virginia's Bill of Rights, rose to say, "It would give great quiet to the people" if the Constitution were prefaced with a bill of rights.

Elbridge Gerry of Massachusetts agreed and moved that a committee start working up such a bill.

The motion was voted down, 10 states to 0. The records reflect no supporters other than Mason and Gerry, who were unable to bring along even their own state delegations. James Madison, father of the Constitution and the man who would later shepherd the Bill of Rights amendments through the first Congress, apparently voted against the idea at the convention.

Why Not?

Why did the framers oppose a bill of rights?

The most human reason that can be suggested is exhaustion. As they prepared to go home to their families and their personal business, the Mason-Gerry proposal could have substantially delayed adjournment. Madison later said haste and fatigue were among the reasons the convention rejected Mason's suggestion.

A higher-minded reason, and one that the framers used later during the ratification debates, was that a bill of rights was unnecessary and might do more harm than good.

The argument went this way: The new federal government was to have only those powers delegated to it by the Constitution. The Constitution gave Congress no authority to regulate speech, press or religion.

As Alexander Hamilton, one of the intractable opponents of a bill of rights, asked in the Federalist Papers: "Why declare that things shall not be done which there is no power to do?"

If you start stating the things that Congress *doesn't* have the power to do, people might become confused and think that it has the power to do everything else. Rather than restraining the power of the federal government, you might add to it.

Bear in mind that the men making this argument preferred a strong national government, even stronger than the one they created. For example, Hamilton had proposed that the governors of the states be appointed by the president. Madison felt strongly that Congress should be able to veto state laws. They restrained themselves out of a sense of what the public would accept.

For these same men to argue that the problem with a bill of rights was that it might inadvertently increase the power of the federal government has a hollow ring.

Mason and Gerry, the two who had proposed a bill of rights, were two of the three members of the convention who refused to sign the Constitution.

Mason announced, according to Madison's notes, "that he would sooner chop off his right hand than put it to the Constitution as it now stands."

In the debates that followed adjournment, members of the convention used a variety of arguments to defend the omission of a bill of rights.

Roger Sherman of Connecticut wrote: "No bill of rights ever yet bound the supreme power longer than the honeymoon of a new married couple, unless the rulers were interested in preserving the rights." In other words, a written bill of rights wouldn't do any good because it could be easily disregarded by a powerful government.

John Dickinson of Delaware wrote that a bill of rights would do as much good as reminding ourselves "that the sun enlightens, warms, invigorates and cheers, or how horrid it would be to have his blessed beams intercepted by our being thrust into mines or dungeons."

Dickinson's argument harks back to the statement in the Declaration of Independence that basic rights are given to men by God. If so, no man can take them away and no man-made document is necessary to guarantee them.

Hamilton, in the Federalist Papers, warned against "the indulgence of an injudicious zeal for bills of rights" and said such a bill "would sound much better in a treatise of ethics than in a constitution of government."

South Carolina delegate C.C. Pinckney gave the most audacious and least appealing justification. He said a bill of rights in the Constitution would have made a hypocrite of slaveowners like himself since bills of rights "generally begin with declaring that all men are by nature born free. Now we should make that declaration with a very bad grace, when a large part of our property consists in men who are actually born slaves."

A SHORT CONSTITUTIONAL

"A bill of rights is what the people are entitled to against every government on earth ... and what no just government should refuse or rest on inference," Thomas Jefferson wrote from Paris to his good friend James Madison in December of 1787.

Jefferson, primary author of the Declaration of Independence, was out of the constitutional action in 1787. He was U.S. ambassador to France. But he received progress reports from Madison.

Jefferson was far less of a nationalist than Madison. He believed that with a few amendments the Articles of Confederation could satisfy the need for a governing document.

When the Philadelphia convention adjourned, Madison rushed a copy of the Constitution to Paris for Jefferson's comments. Jefferson described those parts of the Constitution he liked and then continued, in words so strong and clear that one might almost make a case for Jefferson being the father, in absentia, of the Bill of Rights.

"I will now add what I do not like (about the Constitution). First the omission of a bill of rights providing clearly and without the aid of sophisms for freedom of religion, freedom of the press, protection against standing armies, restriction against monopolies, the eternal and unremitting force of the habeas corpus laws, and trials by jury..."

Madison was beginning to weaken. Having voted against the bill of rights in the convention, he wrote back to Jefferson that such a guarantee might not do any harm (although he still didn't see how it would do much good).

"I have never thought the omission (of a bill of rights from the Constitution) a material defect, nor been anxious to supply it even by subsequent amendment for any other reason than that it is anxiously desired by others," Madison, the future fourth president, wrote to Jefferson, the future third.

But by 1789, when the first Congress met, Madison had become one of the strongest advocates of a bill of rights.

14

Politics and the Birth
of the Bill of Rights

The Bill of Rights was born an orphan, the offspring of a quarrel between two giants of America's founding generation.

James Madison wanted a U.S. Constitution with no bill of rights. He was interested in establishing the power of the federal government over the states and in securing the victory of his faction, the Federalists, over the opponents of the new Constitution.

Patrick Henry wanted to use a bill of rights to preserve state power or, even better in his view, to undermine the Constitution.

The two Virginians slugged out their differences over four years. The battle was characterized more by hardball politics than learned debate.

When the dust settled, the Constitution sported a bill of rights with which neither Madison nor Henry was satisfied but which, 196 years later, has become the most beloved portion of our Constitution.

The paradox is that the guarantee of Americans' individual liberties against government interference was produced by a tug of war between two men, neither of whom was primarily motivated by a concern for individual liberties.

Soon after the Constitutional Convention adjourned, Virginia delegate George Mason published his reasons for refusing to sign the Constitution. His essay began:

"There is no Declaration of Rights, and the laws of the general government being paramount to the laws and constitution of the several States, the Declarations of Rights in the separate States are no security."

Mason's argument touched a nerve. Was this powerful new federal government a threat to the very liberties the Minutemen had fought and bled for?

The issue of the missing bill of rights became the paramount issue of debate during the campaign for ratification.

"A bill of rights may be summed up in a few words," Henry thundered during the Virginia debate on ratification. "What do they tell us? That our rights are reserved. Why not say so? Is it because it will consume too much paper?"

Henry didn't have to answer his sarcastic question. A parchment shortage wasn't the problem. The problem, he said, was that "The rights of conscience, trial by jury, liberty of the press, all your immunities and franchises, all pretensions to human rights and privileges are rendered insecure" by the creation of a powerful new federal government.

It may sound like Mason and Henry are on the same side. Actually, there is a key difference between them that helps clarify the politics of the ratification campaign.

Mason seems to have truly believed that if a bill of rights was added, he could support the proposed new constitution.

While Henry's devotion to rights was sincere, he and other opponents of ratification exploited the issue. Henry was fundamentally opposed to the Constitution. His objections were too numerous to be satisfied by a few amendments.

Henry did not want the federal government to have direct taxing power. (It did not under the Articles of Confederation). He wanted to restrain the new federal power to raise and maintain an army. He objected to the constitutional provision that prohibited states from issuing money or legislating for the relief of debtors.

Henry believed in states' rights, decentralization and the charms of small republics. The proposed new system was too big, too national, too centralized for him.

But of all the Anti-federalist objections to the Constitution, the absence of a bill of rights was the one that garnered the widest support, and Henry was willing to ride whatever horse was available.

During the ratification campaign it became clear that the framers had blundered by omitting a bill of rights. Around that blunder, the anti-ratification campaign strategy was formed.

The Strategies, Pro and Anti

If those (such as Mason) who believed that a bill of rights was necessary, stuck together with those (such as Henry) who were opposed to the whole constitution, they could create a winning coalition, especially in the key state of Virginia.

The Henry faction cleverly decided not to demand a vote *against* ratification. That would be asking too much of the Mason types, who supported the Constitution in general terms.

Instead, Anti-federalists would demand that a bill of rights be added, and try to get the ratification votes made *conditional* on the addition of such a bill. If they won, a second convention would have to be called to frame the bill of rights before the Constitution could go into effect.

Just as the first convention had exceeded its mandate (it was only supposed to propose amendments to the Articles of Confederation, not write a whole new charter), so the second convention might do the same in reverse.

Henry and other Anti-federalists who had boycotted the first convention, or left early, would not make that mistake again. They would stay to make sure that the second convention protected states' power.

The Federalists recognized that their opponents had a powerful campaign issue. Here was their counter-strategy:

Conceding that a bill of rights was needed, they would urge the states to ratify unconditionally while *recommending* amendments to secure rights.

Once the Constitution was safely adopted, they promised, rights amendments would receive high priority from the first Congress.

The strategy and counter-strategy emerged during the Massachusetts ratifying convention. The recommended amendments turned out to be crucial in narrowly bringing Massachusetts into the union.

It worked again for Madison and the Federalists on a narrow vote at the Virginia convention. The Constitution was ratified and the bill of rights became the first campaign promise in constitutional history.

Henry and the Anti-federalists would have opportunities for revenge, and they would seize them.

Mr. Madison Runs for Congress

Under the new Constitution, the state legislatures were to elect the U.S. senators. That meant that Henry, the pre-eminent power in Virginia politics, could name that state's senators.

So the state that had contributed so much to the writing of the Constitution sent as its first U.S. senators two Henry allies who opposed the Constitution. The Federalist they defeated was Madison.

For Madison to go to Congress, he would have to be elected to the House.

Madison wrote to an ally that he hoped "the arrangements for the popular elections may secure me against any competition which would require on my part any step that would speak a solicitude which I do not feel, or have the appearance of a spirit of electioneering which I despise."

In other words, Madison would accept a House seat. But he hoped the drawing of the House districts would provide him a district so safe he wouldn't even have to even ask for the job, let alone campaign for it.

Fat chance, with Henry and the Anti-federalist Legislature drawing up the districts.

In what was presumably the first case of gerrymandering under the new Constitution (one historian likes to call it Henrymandering), they constructed a lopsided House district grouping Madison's home county with seven Anti-federalist counties.

Madison's district also was populated heavily by Baptists, who made up a large minority in Virginia. All this talk about the new Constitution endangering basic freedoms, including protection for religious minorities, had the Baptists nervous.

Madison had always supported religious liberty. But to hear the Anti-federalists tell it, this guy Madison opposed any constitutional amendments, including one to secure freedom of religion.

As a final annoyance, the Anti-federalists supported James Monroe for the House seat, the same Monroe who would eventually be Madison's secretary of state and later fifth president of the United States. That's right, "Monroe Doctrine" Monroe.

Much as Madison may have believed that the seat was his due, he had to break down and actually campaign for it. Even more humiliating, he would have to campaign on a pledge to amend his beloved Constitution the first chance he got.

"It is my sincere opinion that the Constitution ought to be revised," he wrote to a Baptist minister in a letter intended for public circulation, "and that the first Congress ... ought to prepare and recommend to the States ... the most satisfactory provisions for all essential rights, particularly the rights of Conscience in the fullest latitude ..."

Madison won the seat.

Mr. Madison Writes the Rights

The first Congress faced a mind-boggling array of tasks. The Constitution provided no executive departments and only the idea of a judiciary. Although the charter granted the power to raise taxes, Congress had to decide what taxes, how much and how to collect them, and other matters a bit weightier than the 55-mile-per-hour speed limit.

So, naturally, on March 4, 1789, the day Congress opened by constitutional mandate, only 21 of the 81 members were present and no business could be transacted for about a month until more folks showed up.

The House had a quorum but had not accomplished any of those basic tasks by June 8 when U.S. Rep. James Madison (Fed.-Va.) rose to ask for consideration of constitutional amendments to secure basic liberties.

Some felt the Congress should wait a year or two and see how the new system worked before deciding how to change it. But Madison stood firm. He had voted against a bill of rights in the convention. He had argued later that such a bill was unnecessary. Now he said he could tolerate no delay.

Let's pause a moment to consider the conversion of Madison from opponent to sponsor of the Bill of Rights.

First, it may be that Thomas Jefferson's letters had taken their toll. Jefferson had argued in letters to his friend Madison that "A bill of rights is what the people are entitled to against every government on earth ... and what no just government should refuse." Madison adopted Jefferson's position and many of his arguments.

Second, Madison had a campaign promise to fulfill. The Baptist vote back in his district may have been on his mind when he announced in Congress: "I considered myself bound in honor and in duty to" press for the rights amendments.

Third, as a leading Federalist, Madison was anxious to rebut the idea that the Anti-federalists were the friends of rights and freedom and that his was the party of tyranny and oppression. As he told the House:

"It will be a desirable thing to extinguish from the bosom of every member of the community, any apprehensions that there are those among his countrymen who wish to deprive them of the liberty for which they valiantly fought and honorably bled."

Fourth and perhaps most convincing, if there must be a bill of rights, Madison wanted to control what was in it.

Henry Never Quit

The movement for a second constitutional convention hadn't died. The Virginia Legislature, led by Henry, had called for a second convention to draft satisfactory amendments. The resolution listed, among the amendments, a restriction on federal taxing power.

Such a convention, if called, might go a lot further than guaranteeing freedom of expression and the right to a fair trial.

The surest way to quiet the calls for a new convention was to pass a bill of rights stealing from the opposition's list the most popular but least threatening amendments.

One of Madison's House allies put it this way: "I venture to affirm that unless you take early notice of this subject, you will not have power to deliberate. The people will clamor for a new convention; they will not trust the House any longer."

And Madison was successful. With one major exception, the amendments he drafted were very close to the ones Congress approved. The exception was this: Madison proposed an amendment that would bind the *states* to respect freedom of conscience and speech and the right to a jury trial in criminal cases.

If adopted, this would have been the only provision in the Bill of Rights limiting state governments. Madison argued that this was "the most valuable amendment in the whole list." But it was killed in the Senate. As a result, the states remained free to interfere with free speech, trial by jury and other rights, which they did until well into the 20th century.

By Sept. 25, 1789, the Bill of Rights had passed both houses and was referred to the states for ratification. Ten states were needed. Nine ratified quickly. Fittingly it was Virginia, where the Madison-Henry rivalry continued to play out, that stalled ratification.

Henry's ally, U.S. Sen. William Grayson, wrote to him that the proposed amendments "are good for nothing, and I believe, as many others do, that they will do more harm than benefit."

Henry denounced the amendments as "guileful," and said they would do no more than "lull suspicion." They did that sufficiently that Henry was unable to defeat them.

The Virginia Anti-federalists held up the final outcome for 18 more months, then granted the key ratification, and the 10 amendments took effect Dec. 15, 1791.

15

The Bill of Rights' Century of Slumber

The Bill of Rights, guaranteeing freedom of religion, took effect in 1791. So how come Massachusetts had an established state religion — supported by tax dollars — until 1833? How come Jews couldn't vote in Rhode Island until 1841?

The Bill of Rights supposedly guaranteed freedom of the press. So why was the *New York Tribune* banned from being mailed into Virginia in 1859? Why was a North Carolina man convicted of the crime of circulating a book?

The Bill of Rights says "freedom of speech." The U.S. Supreme Court said as late as 1922 that "The Constitution of the United States imposes upon the states no obligation to . . . the right of free speech."

According to the mythic view of the Constitution, the Bill of Rights should have protected Americans against violations of such basic freedoms.

Yet well into the 20th century, some Americans were denied freedom of expression, the right to jury trials and fundamental stuff like that.

What's going on here?

The answer is simple: The Bill of Rights didn't apply to the states. As a result, it was scarcely worth the parchment it was written on for about a century after it became the law of the land.

Most of the Bill of Rights has now been interpreted as applying to the states, but the process has been gradual and is still incomplete. For most of the history of this country, the situation on civil liberties was this:

Congress was forbidden to abridge free speech, press, religion and all. The state legislatures could abridge them (unless prohibited by their state constitutions) — and they did.

You were entitled to a fair, speedy, public jury trial, to confront your accusers; you couldn't be forced to incriminate yourself, etc. — if your case was in federal court. If your case was in state court (as most were), you had no such guarantees. It wasn't until 1969 — that's right, 1969 — that the Supreme Court held that the defendants couldn't be tried twice for the same offense in state courts.

Why Didn't It Apply?

The idea that the Bill of Rights didn't cover the states wasn't illogical. The rights amendments, written primarily by James Madison in the first Congress, was the product of a debate about states' rights and the limits of the new federal authority.

The amendments adopted were a concession to those who felt that the new federal government had too much power *compared with the states.* Madison, an advocate of strong central government, had tried to put through an amendment requiring the states to respect basic civil liberties, but the Senate wouldn't go along.

We don't know much about the Senate's reasons because at the time the Senate met in closed, secret sessions.

The First Amendment, which contains several of the key civil liberties, reads as follows:

"Congress shall make no law respecting an establishment of religion, or prohibiting the free exercise thereof; or abridging the freedom of speech, or of the press, or the right of the people peaceably to assemble, and to petition the Government for a redress of grievances."

Although Congress couldn't make such laws, the states could.

The rest of the rights amendments don't specify whether they apply to Congress or the states. The question remained open until 1833, when the Supreme Court decided Barron vs. Baltimore.

Barron's Wharf

John Barron owned a lucrative wharf in Baltimore until a city street-grading project changed the shape of the waterfront, creating shoals and shallows that rendered Barron's wharf worthless.

The Fifth Amendment says no one shall be deprived of his property without due process of law, "nor shall private property be taken for public use without just compensation." Barron said he lost his property but when he demanded compensation, the city of Baltimore told him to take a long walk off a short wharf. Barron appealed to the Supreme Court on the grounds that the city had violated his Fifth Amendment rights.

Unlike the First Amendment, the Fifth doesn't specify whether it applies to Congress or the states or both. In the Barron ruling, the court settled the question so clearly and broadly that it covered all the rights in the Bill of Rights and pretty much knocked individual liberties off the court docket for 100 years.

The decision said: "Had the framers of these Amendments (the Bill of Rights) intended them to be limitations on the powers of the state governments, they would have ... expressed that intention."

Ironically, the decision was rendered by Chief Justice John Marshall, who in most of his famous decisions was regarded as the great champion of national power, especially the power of the federal government over the states. But when it came to protecting individual rights against attacks by state or local governments, Marshall decided, the federal courts were helpless.

The most outrageous instances of states violating individual liberties before the Civil War were laws by slave states attempting to restrict speaking, publishing or meeting about abolition.

In 1836 Virginia made it a serious crime to "advocate or advise the abolition of slavery."

In Louisiana it was illegal to speak or publish language that might produce discontent among free blacks or insubordination among slaves.

A North Carolina man was convicted and sentenced to a year in prison for the crime of circulating the book "The Impending Crisis," an attack on slavery that Republicans used as a campaign document.

The defendant argued that he had only circulated the book among whites, but the state Supreme Court ruled that a book that had a tendency "to cause slaves to be discontented and free negroes dissatisfied" was illegal whether circulated among blacks or whites.

State laws required postmasters to screen incoming mail for publications "denying the right of masters to property in their slaves and inculcating the duty of resistance to such a right." It was under one of those laws that a Virginia postmaster banned the New York Tribune in 1859.

Most of these laws were not challenged before the U.S. Supreme Court, but they didn't have to be. The court had already announced in the Baltimore wharf case that states could constitutionally trample the individual civil liberties of their citizens. When the court did handle such a case, the result was always consistent with that principle.

There the matter stood until after the Civil War. The post-war Congress attempted to solve the problem with the 14th Amendment, which would overrule the Barron decision and the original intent of the framers.

The amendment, ratified in 1868, said three ways that state government had to respect individual liberties. It said: 1. No state could abridge the privileges and immunities of U.S. citizens. 2. No state could deprive a citizen of life, liberty or property without due process. 3. All citizens were entitled to equal protection of the laws.

But over the hundred years that followed, the Supreme Court applied the Bill of Rights to the states only haltingly and on a piecemeal basis. By now, most — but not all — of the rights in the Bill of Rights have been applied to the states.

A SHORT CONSTITUTIONAL

No image of the Constitution at work is more heroic than that of the Supreme Court rising with black-robed dignity to defend the right of an American under the First Amendment to speak or publish his thoughts and opinions.

Curiously, for the first century and a quarter after the First Amendment was ratified this happened exactly zero times. In fact, the high court didn't handle a freedom of expression case before World War I.

Under the doctrine announced in Barron vs. Baltimore, the Supreme Court could get involved only if *Congress* adopted a law abridging freedom of speech or press.

This did happen once, when the First Amendment was just seven years old. But the Supreme Court didn't do anything about it.

The Sedition Act of 1798 made it a crime, punishable by a fine and imprisonment, to publish "false, scandalous or malicious writing" bringing into disrepute the government, Congress or the president "or to excite against them the hatred of the good people of the United States."

In the highly partisan political context of the time, the law was clearly an attempt by Federalist President John Adams and the Federalist Congress to repress criticism of themselves by Thomas Jefferson's Democratic-Republicans. Ten men, all of them Republican printers or editors, were convicted under the law.

The Supreme Court never considered the constitutionality of the law. But the individual justices presided over the trials of the sedition cases. (In those days, Supreme Court justices rode a circuit and functioned as ordinary federal judges in their districts.)

In those cases, the justices not only upheld the sedition law, they refused to allow defense lawyers to challenge its constitutionality. And the justices conducted the trials in a highly partisan manner, browbeating witnesses and speechifying to the jury on behalf of the Federalist Party.

Ironically, the Sedition Act, which was intended to help the Federalists hang onto power, was extremely unpopular and helped Jefferson beat Adams in the election of 1800.

When Jefferson took office, the hated law had expired. He granted presidential pardons to the 10 members of his party convicted under the law. A few years later, the Jeffersonian-controlled Congress reimbursed, with interest, all those who had been fined under the law. And Congress later tried, unsuccess-

fully, to impeach Supreme Court Justice Samuel Chase, whose conduct while presiding over sedition trials had been the most partisan.

Leonard W. Levy, a leading historian of the Bill of Rights, has argued in several works that the doctrine of a free press that prevails in the United States was established during the argument over the Sedition Act.

When the Bill of Rights took effect in 1791, freedom of the press meant the government couldn't stop you in advance from publishing your views, but it could prosecute you afterward for publishing harsh criticism of the government. (Such writings were called seditious libel.)

Neither Jefferson, the leading American libertarian of the time, nor Madison, the primary author of the First Amendment, had suggested before 1798 that citizens had a right to criticize the government with impunity. The most liberal view was that you should be acquitted of sedition if you could prove that what you had written was true.

This liberal view was incorporated into the Sedition Act of 1798, which sought to punish only "false" publications that brought the government into disrepute.

But during the debate over the Sedition Act a new doctrine took shape. If what you were expressing was a political opinion, truth or falsity weren't always relevant concepts.

"There are many truths, important to society, which are not susceptible of that full, direct and positive evidence which alone can be exhibited before a court and a jury," wrote one Democratic-Republican pamphleteer in 1799.

"It would seem a mockery to say that no laws shall be passed preventing publications from being made, but that laws might be passed for punishing them in case they should be made," wrote Madison.

If this was to be a free country, the new doctrine said, Americans must be allowed to criticize the government, no matter how harshly, even if the criticisms are scandalous, irresponsible and false. In short, the existence of the crime of seditious libel was inconsistent with a system in which the people are sovereign over the government rather than vice versa.

16

The Second Constitution

This bulletin just in: 1987 was not the bicentennial of the U.S. Constitution.

Our sacred national charter is really only 119 years old. It was written by a bunch of guys you've never heard of whose motives were a combination of high morality and low partisan politics. It was ratified under duress and didn't take effect until this century.

Okay, so maybe I exaggerated a tad to get your attention. The blasphemy above has more than a grain of truth to it. Let's take it a grain at a time.

Grain of Truth No. 1: The Constitution We Live by Today was Born in 1868.

U.S. Supreme Court Justice Thurgood Marshall, in a 1987 speech criticizing the bicentennial hoopla, said: "While the Union survived the Civil War, the Constitution did not. In its place arose a new, more promising basis for justice and equality." He was talking about the 14th Amendment, ratified in 1868.

Before the 14th Amendment, the Constitution did not guarantee the equality of individuals before the law and had no impact on civil rights.

Most of what 20th-century Americans view as the noble influence of the Constitution derives from the 14th Amendment.

Desegregation, the guarantee of a fair trial, the legal rights of women — none of these could have been accomplished under the Constitution as it stood at the end of the Civil War. Even the abolition of slavery by the 13th Amendment in 1865 was a hollow victory for Southern blacks until the 14th Amendment gave it meaning.

Yet the amendment was a product of constitutional, political and military chaos. Before we continue the grain-by-grain analysis, here's a summary of the situation that gave rise to the framing of the amendment.

The Civil War had just ended. Eleven Southern states were occupied by Union military forces and ruled by presidentially appointed governments.

Congress considered these governments unready for readmission to Congress, but by a breathtaking double standard, Congress allowed the un-states to ratify the 13th Amendment abolishing slavery.

Congress didn't have much choice. The Constitution requires three-fourths of the states to ratify an amendment. Some Confederate states would be needed even if all Union states ratified. (They didn't. Kentucky and Delaware, two of the slave states that had stayed in the Union, rejected the amendment.)

Thus the great moral blot of legalized slavery was exorcised from the Constitution by these questionable means on Dec. 6, 1865. (If the 15 slave states had stuck together, they could have blocked such an amendment until there were at least 60 states.)

Southern legislatures replaced their proslavery laws with so-called "black codes." Under the guise of regulating apprenticeship or outlawing vagrancy, the laws gave blacks little choice but to continue working the farms of their former masters.

In Mississippi, for example, freedmen had to bind themselves to a one-year term of labor. The worker's entire wage would be forfeited if he tried to leave during the year.

Presumably an employer could arrange that by year's end the worker owed more than the wages he was due. He would have to bind himself for another year or, if he left without his wages, take his chances with the penal codes as a "vagrant."

Sentences included corporal punishment, limited to two hours a day of being suspended by one's thumbs. For many crimes, the penal codes provided harsher punishments for blacks than for whites.

In short, the black codes continued slavery under other names. (Many Northern states had similar racist laws.)

Other aspects of the codes restricted blacks' privilege of owning weapons, buying property, filing lawsuits, assembling and traveling. Such state laws were constitutional under Barron vs. Baltimore. In 1857 (the Dred Scott decision), the court ruled that even a free black could never be a U.S. citizen.

These were among the problems Congress addressed with the 14th Amendment.

Grain of Truth No. 2: The Framers of the 14th Amendment were a Bunch of Guys you Never Heard of.

Does the name John A. Bingham ring a bell?

Section 1 of the amendment, which contains all the good stuff, was written primarily by Congressman Bingham of Ohio. If fairness had anything to do with historical reputations, Bingham would be known as the father of the second Constitution.

Other major players included Rep. Thaddeus Stevens of Pennsylvania, Sens. Ben Wade of Ohio, Jacob Howard of Michigan and William Fessenden of Maine, Senate chairman of the joint Reconstruction Committee, which drafted the amendment.

All of the men named above were Republicans. This is no coincidence. The 14th was very much a Republican amendment. One of its purposes was to safeguard Republican control of the government.

The Republican Party didn't even exist before 1854. Six years later it elected a president and was the dominant party in the North but virtually nonexistent in the South. (Many Southern states kept Abraham Lincoln's name off the ballot in 1860.) In 1861 the region dominated by Democrats seceded, leaving the GOP (better make that Grand Young Party) with a huge majority in Congress.

By an enormous Catch-22, the South stood to *gain* power in Congress by the abolition of slavery. Under the original Constitution, a slave counted three-fifths as much as a free person in calculating the number of seats each state got in Congress.

With slavery abolished, the ex-Confederate states would get full credit for their black populations, creating a bunch of congressional seats, presumably to be filled by Democrats.

Small wonder that the Republican Congress was in no hurry to readmit the Southern states. Nor that it developed a strong interest in giving the vote to the freed Southern blacks, who would presumably be Republicans.

But don't assume that enthusiasm for black voting rights was widespread in the North. Many Northern states limited the vote to whites.

During the Civil War the abolitionist cause had gained popularity in the North as a military measure — not because of any widespread commitment to racial equality.

Northern Democrats in the 1860's campaigned against black suffrage, and warned that the Republicans were going to let blacks vote. Republicans were anxious to avoid handing their opponents a campaign issue.

Grain No. 3: Their Motives were a Mixture of High Morality and Low Partisan Politics.

Okay, here's a quick recap of some of the moral, legal and political problems Congress was trying to solve with the 14th Amendment.

■ The Dred Scott decision said blacks couldn't be U.S. citizens.

■ Barron vs. Baltimore said the Bill of Rights didn't apply to the states.

■ The black codes discriminated overtly against the ex-slaves and continued slavery under other names.

■ President Andrew Johnson insisted on the immediate readmission of the Southern states, but Congress wanted to delay it until Republican control could be assured.

■ Congress wanted to enfranchise Southern blacks, whom they figured would vote Republican, without enfranchising Northern blacks, for fear of alienating white voters in their own states.

Here's what Section 1 of the 14th Amendment said:

■ Everyone born or naturalized in the United States is a citizen, overruling the Dred Scott decision.

■ No state can abridge the privileges and immunities of U.S. citizens. (Does this mean the Bill of Rights applies to the states? That's been debated ever since.)

■ Due-process rights had to be respected by the states.

■ Every person in a state is entitled to "equal protection of the laws," so the black codes, which explicitly treated people differently based on their race, would be unconstitutional.

Section 2 dealt with the problem of the disappearing three-fifths rule. Any state that disfranchised its blacks would have its representation in the House reduced proportionately to the number of adult males it deprived of voting privileges.

Northern states had small black populations. Disfranchising them wouldn't cost seats in Congress, but the Southern states would have to choose between letting blacks vote or forfeiting 20-some congressional seats.

Grain No. 4: It was Ratified under Duress.

The amendment needed ratification from 27 of the 36 states to become law. In 1866, 10 of the 11 ex-Confederate states rejected it by huge margins (as did Maryland and Delaware, two ex-slave states that hadn't seceded.) Like the 13th Amendment, the 14th was sunk without Southern ratifications.

In March of 1867, Congress passed, over Johnson's veto, An Act for the More Efficient Government of the Rebel States, which laid out the terms for restoring ex-Confederate states to full rights.

Among the conditions: They had to adopt new state constitutions guaranteeing black suffrage (thus underscoring the double standard: Southerners had to let blacks vote; Northerners didn't). And they had to ratify the 14th Amendment.

When the framers of the 1787 Constitution drafted Article V laying out the rules for amendments, they never intended for any state to have to ratify with a gun to its head. But that's literally and figuratively what happened to the Southern states.

The figurative gun was the threat that they would not be readmitted until they ratified the 14th Amendment. The literal gun was that until restored to normal statehood, they would continue to be governed under martial law.

Given this choice, the Southern states reconsidered the amendment and found it more, ahem, attractive.

Grain No. 5: It Didn't Take Effect Until this century.

The 14th Amendment took effect July 9, 1868, but the version of the 14th Amendment that matches our mythical view of the Constitution didn't really emerge until this century.

Clause by clause, the Supreme Court, Congress and the states stripped the amendment of its libertarian and egalitarian potential during most of the amendment's life.

The "privileges and immunities" clause was interpreted so narrowly that it lost any meaning. "Due process" almost met a similar fate until the court finally used the language to apply the Bill of Rights to the states in the 1930's and 1960's. That story is told at greater length in the 18th essay of this book: "The Rights Come to Life."

"Equal protection" was subverted into the doctrine of "separate but equal." Under that doctrine, segregated societies were fully constitutional. Not until 1954 did the Supreme Court discover that "equal protection" required desegregation. That is the subject of the 20th essay.

The provision to reduce the congressional representation of a state that denied the vote to blacks was never enforced. Many states used various means to disfranchise black voters until the 1960's. None ever lost any congressional seats for it.

A SHORT CONSTITUTIONAL

Here's your chance to be a constitutional scholar.

After reading the excerpt below, you have to answer one of the most important and persistent questions the Supreme Court has dealt with in the past 120 years: Did the primary author of the 14th Amendment intend to apply the Bill of Rights to the states?

Just before the 1866 vote in the U.S. House, this is what the author, Rep. John Bingham of Ohio, told his colleagues:

"The necessity for the first section of this amendment to the Constitution, Mr. Speaker, is one of the lessons that have been taught to your committee and taught to all the people of this country by the history of the past four years of terrific conflict (the Civil War) - that history in which God is, and in which He teaches the profoundest lessons to men and nations.

"There was a want hitherto, and there remains a want now, in the Constitution of our country, which the proposed amendment will supply. What is that? It is the power in the people, the whole people of the United States, by express authority of the Constitution to do that by congressional enactment which hitherto they have not had the power to do, and have never attempted to do; that is, to protect by national law the privileges and immunities of all the citizens of the republic and the inborn rights of every person within its jurisdiction whenever the same shall be abridged or denied by the unconstitutional acts of any state."

So far, although Bingham sounds like a bit of a blowhard, it does seem that he's leading up to saying that the Bill of Rights should apply to the states. But here comes a curve:

"Allow me, Mr. Speaker, in passing to say that this amendment takes from no state any right that ever pertained to it. No state ever had the right, under the forms of law or otherwise, to deny to any freeman the equal protection of the laws or to abridge the privileges and immunities of any citizen of the Republic, although many of them have assumed and exercised the power, and that without remedy."

But the states until then did have the right to violate the Bill of Rights, as the courts had repeatedly ruled. Bingham, a lawyer, cited one of the most important of those decisions in arguing for the amendment.

In the same speech, Bingham mentioned "cruel and unusual punishments" as the sort of abuse he wants to correct. The prohibition against such punishments is part of the Bill of Rights.

But Bingham also said in another speech that if this amendment had been in place earlier, the Civil War would have been prevented. It is hard, though not impossible, to imagine how Bingham felt the Bill of Rights could have prevented the Confederate states from seceding.

Now, is it clear to you what Bingham intended? Or is it more clear why historians and lawyers ever since have been able to have their way with Bingham and his colleagues?

17

What Does a Guy Have to Do to Get Impeached Around Here?

In the spring of 1987, as the Iran-Contra mess unfolded, a few constitutional gurus suggested that just possibly President Reagan had committed an impeachable offense by causing or allowing that weird scheme to be hatched and implemented from within his White House.

The suggestion quickly died, mortally wounded by two mysteries.

The first was what acts of misfeasance, malfeasance or nonfeasance Reagan had committed. No one has ever figured it out.

The second was a constitutional question that hadn't been kicked around since Richard Nixon resigned one step ahead of the impeachers: How badly does a president have to screw up before he can be sacked by Congress?

The short answer is we don't know because it has never happened. Besides Nixon, the only other close call was in 1868. President Andrew Johnson was impeached by the House. (Impeachment is actually first part of the process. The House impeaches, which causes the Senate to hold a trial. Conviction by a two-thirds vote of the Senate would remove a president from office.)

In Johnson's case, the Senate came within one vote of removing him. What were Johnson's high crimes and misdemeanors?

He fired a member of his Cabinet.

That's right. Johnson came that close to the ultimate constitutional defeat for doing something other presidents could do legally.

But when Johnson did it in 1867, it was illegal. Congress had passed a law prohibiting the president from firing federal officials unless the Senate approved.

On first hearing, this sounds like a Congress run amok, trampling the legitimate power of the president. The impeachment has

traditionally been characterized as an unjust and politically motivated action by a power-crazed Congress.

An odor of partisanship and vindictiveness does waft from the
incident. For example, the impeachment was by a straight party-
line vote. And Rep. Ben Butler, a leader of the so-called Radical
Republicans, was so hungry for high crimes that he negotiated
with a convicted perjurer who offered to provide evidence linking
Johnson to the assassination of Abraham Lincoln.

But the Johnson case raises more complex questions that get to
the heart of the constitutional balance of powers and highlight a
major difference between our system and the parliamentary forms
of democracy that prevail elsewhere.

Reconstruction Riddle

Johnson was a self-educated Tennessee tailor who, as a U.S.
senator in 1861, was the only Southern senator to remain loyal to
the Union during the Civil War. A lifelong Democrat, Johnson
hadn't even voted for Republican Lincoln in 1860. But Lincoln
rewarded Johnson's loyalty by taking him as a running mate in the
election of 1864, the only instance since the emergence of presidential tickets that the running mates were from different parties.
They won and were inaugurated in March of 1865.

Six weeks later, John Wilkes Booth made Johnson president.

Johnson inherited an overwhelmingly Northern Republican
Congress and a whopping constitutional conundrum. The Civil
War ended during Johnson's first weeks in office. On what terms
would the 11 seceded states be readmitted to the Union? The
Constitution itself offered no guidance.

Johnson said the president should call the shots. He offered
prompt readmission on generous terms (closely following the
strategy Lincoln had outlined).

Congress wanted more concessions from the Southerners, and
was willing to keep the ex-Confederate states out of Congress until
they complied.

In 1867, Congress passed a bill dividing the South into five
districts, governed by Union generals under martial law. To be
restored to full rights, a Southern state had to adopt a new
constitution guaranteeing voting rights for the freed slaves, and
had to ratify the proposed 14th Amendment, guaranteeing citizenship, due process rights and equal protection for the freedmen.

Johnson, a former slaveowner, accepted the abolition of slavery.

But he was a virulent racist. He opposed voting rights for blacks, whom he called "corrupt in principle," "enemies of free institutions" and incapable of participating in democracy. He opposed the 14th Amendment.

He vetoed the 1867 law. Congress overrode the veto. But as commander-in-chief of the Army, the president could appoint the military governors. He appointed generals who shared his views on the proper relationship between the races and fired those who ran their districts from a civil rights perspective.

Cold War

This was typical of the cold war between the president and Congress during the period. Johnson vetoed all major reconstruction bills, and Congress overrode the vetoes. Johnson then used his executive powers to thwart the intentions of the congressional laws.

He used his appointment powers, his power to grant pardons, his power to fire officials and the power every president has to set a tone for the national government. He couldn't have his way on reconstruction. So he found means to keep Congress from having its way.

By similar methods, Johnson thwarted Congress' effort to chop up confiscated Southern plantations into 40-acre plots and distribute ownership to the former slaves.

The more ways Johnson found to circumvent Congress, the more laws Congress passed to force his cooperation. Then Johnson sought further ways of frustrating the new laws.

Perhaps most important, during this critical period, with the future of civil rights and race relations hanging in the balance, Johnson inspired his fellow white Southerners to an attitude of resistance.

Congress became more desperate. Impeachment talk started. Johnson had avoided technical violations of the law. Radical Republicans argued that the president didn't have to commit an indictable crime to be impeached. On the theory that the House could define "high crimes and misdemeanors" to mean a refusal to faithfully execute the acts of Congress, the House Judiciary Committee in late 1867 recommended impeaching Johnson for obstructing the congressional reconstruction program.

The committee alleged no crimes and the impeachment bill failed in the House.

Johnson continued to use the powers of the presidency to defeat the congressional program. In one five-month period, he fired 1,352 postmasters around the country who were loyal Republicans and were not sympathetic to Johnson's policies.

Okay, said Congress, if you're going to fire people who support us, we'll pass a law forbidding you from firing people. The Tenure of Office Act (passed, naturally, over Johnson's veto) said that if the president wanted to fire anyone from a federal appointment requiring Senate confirmation, he had to have Senate concurrence.

The law included special language on Cabinet members as a result of a compromise between the House and Senate, but the meaning was cloudy.

(The Tenure Act was not as blatantly unconstitutional as you might think. The Constitution says nothing about whether the president can fire his appointees after the Senate has confirmed them. The First Congress in 1789 authorized President George Washington to fire his secretary of state, but left vague whether the president got this power directly from the Constitution or from Congress, in which case a later Congress could take it away.)

The Tenure Act was similar in several ways to the Boland Amendment, which was violated in the Iran-Contra mess. Both prohibited the president from doing something (firing his own appointees, or authorizing covert aid to the Nicaraguan Contras) that the president normally did without specific congressional authorization.

Both were unclear in some applications. (Were actions by the president to raise Contra aid from private or foreign donors covered by the Boland Amendment? Were Cabinet appointments excepted from the Tenure Act?) And neither law was a criminal statute in the sense that you could be fined or sent to prison for violations.

While Congress was out of session in the summer of 1867, Johnson suspended Secretary of War Edwin Stanton, a holdover from the Lincoln cabinet. When the Senate returned that winter, Johnson asked, as the Tenure Act required, that the suspension be made permanent. The Senate refused. Stanton was reinstated in January of 1868.

The Overt Act

On Feb. 21, Johnson fired Stanton with a written notice stating that he was acting under his constitutional powers as president (implicitly rejecting the Tenure Act). He also appointed a new secretary, without seeking Senate approval, which was illegal even without the Tenure Act.

Upon learning of Johnson's action, Sen. Charles Sumner of Massachusetts, a leading Johnson adversary, sent a one-word telegram to Stanton: "Stick."

Stanton stuck, spending the night in his office and sending for soldiers to protect against any armed attempt to remove him.

In the House, Rep. John Covode of Pennsylvania didn't bother with telegrams. He moved immediately for a vote impeaching Johnson. It was a Friday afternoon. The House impeached Johnson on Monday, by a vote of 128-47, without even drawing up articles of impeachment. (They were drawn up afterward.)

The one and only trial of a sitting president occurred in the Senate between March 30 and May 26, 1868.

There were questions about whether the Tenure Act covered Cabinet members, or if it did, whether it covered a holdover appointee from a previous president, or whether Johnson really violated the law or was just trying to force a court case so he could test the constitutionality of the law, or whether it was an impeachable offense.

In the end, the Senate vote 35-19 to remove Johnson — one vote short of the two-thirds required by the Constitution.

No Confidence

What would have happened if, instead of being president of the United States, Johnson had been a prime minister under the sort of parliamentary systems that predominate in Europe, Canada and elsewhere?

In those systems, the prime minister is chosen by the majority party or a coalition in parliament. As a condition of keeping his job, he must retain the political support of the majority. He doesn't have to commit a felony to be removed. If he can't get his major legislation through the House, he will lose a so-called vote of confidence and he must resign.

Sometimes new elections are called, sometimes the majority party just changes leaders. The prime minister gets his power from the legislative majority, and they can take it away. Under such a system, Johnson would have lost his job in a Minnesota minute.

But the president of the United States gets his mandate directly from the people, and he gets an almost unbreakable four-year lease on the Oval Office.

To remove him, the majority of the House and two-thirds of the Senate must agree that he committed "treason, bribery or other high crimes and misdemeanors."

The Constitution doesn't offer much guidance on the level of impropriety required. The members of Congress have to be guided by the unwritten or mythic portions of the Constitution.

History indicates that the level of screw-up required is extremely high. You can't impeach a president for losing the support of the congressional majority. Many times (like now, for instance) the president's party is in the minority in Congress (a virtual impossibility in a parliamentary system). This has brought periods of governmental stalemate, but not impeachment.

According to precedent, you can't impeach a president for breaking his campaign promises, nor for blundering into foreign quagmires, nor for appointing people who turn out to be crooks. (You can impeach them, but not him.)

The case of Andrew Johnson, contrary to the traditional view, can be taken as an illustration of just how much a president can get away with under our Constitution, and still keep his job.

A president, obliged to execute the acts of Congress, used every constitutional power of his office to thwart Congress. In the wake of our greatest crisis, as the nation struggled with the urgent task of reconciliation between the regions and between the races, a president brought that process to a standstill for three years.

And when the president broke the law, albeit in a small and technical way, the congressional majority reached for its ultimate constitutional weapon against a president.

And came up one vote short.

The close brush with removal sobered all parties to the dispute. Johnson relaxed his campaign of obstruction. All but three of the seceded states complied with congressional requirements and were restored to full rights by the end of 1868. The following year, Johnson was replaced by Ulysses S. Grant.

Johnson returned to Tennessee, a hero for his defense of white supremacy. He was reelected to the U.S. Senate in 1874. When he died in 1875, he was buried with his head resting on a copy of the Constitution.

A SHORT CONSTITUTIONAL

Andrew Johnson's presidency may have been saved, inadvertently, by one of his fiercest opponents: Sen. Benjamin Wade, a blunt and boisterous radical who, as president pro tem of the Senate, was next in line to be president if Johnson had been removed.

Wade scared the pants off of conservatives, and plenty of others who held the prevailing racist and sexist views of 1868. The idea of the fiery Ohio Republican as president may have been too much even for some who would like to have removed Johnson.

Wade took radical positions on every policy question of the time. He advocated black suffrage and even women's suffrage. If he hadn't thought his wife had enough sense to vote, he liked to say, he wouldn't have married her.

He favored debtors over creditors, high tariff (rejecting the sacred capitalist doctrine of free trade) and predicted that the next great issue would be the inequitable distribution of property between rich and poor, between the hard-working laborers and the lazy bosses.

"If you dullheads can't see this," the ever-diplomatic Wade said in an 1867 speech, "the women will, and will act accordingly."

18

The Rights Come to Life

It wasn't until two spurts of Supreme Court decisions in the 1930's and the 1960's that the constitutional rights of individuals were guaranteed against intrusion by state and local governments.

What difference does it make when we got them, you might ask, as long as we have them now?

If our rights had been carved into the explicit language of the Constitution 200 years ago by George Washington and James Madison, they would by now have survived so many challenges and be so closely associated with the revered founders of the Republic that their durability would be hard to question.

But if guarantees of our precious individual liberties against government invasion were interpreted into the Constitution 20 to 60 years ago by controversial Supreme Court decisions employing murky and shifting legal and historical justifications, how confident can we be that such guarantees won't be interpreted back out?

In fact, U.S. Attorney General Edwin Meese has complained long and loud against the basic doctrine by which the Supreme Court brought the states under the Bill of Rights. Meese says that the court has strayed too far from the original intentions of the framers.

The 14th Amendment, ratified in 1868, says the states can't "abridge the privileges and immunities of citizens of the U.S." and can't "deprive any person of life, liberty or property, without due process of law."

Lawyers and historians have argued ever since about whether the authors meant to apply the Bill of Rights to the states.

But in our system, the Supreme Court gets to say what words in the Constitution mean. Eventually, the court found that most of the Bill of Rights lurked somewhere within the 14th Amendment. It was so well hidden, however, that the court couldn't find it for several decades.

In 1873, the court interpreted the "privileges and immunities" clause within an inch of its life. The justices decided that only a few minuscule rights — such as the right to be protected while traveling on the high seas — were covered. Other more basic rights — such as free speech and fair trial — would continue to be regulated by the states as they saw fit.

It was close — a 5-4 vote. One dissenter eloquently protested that the court was turning "what was meant to be bread into a stone." But after that decision, the privileges and immunities clause did sink like a stone and has scarcely been heard of since.

Over the 50 years, the "due process" clause almost met the same fate.

How Much Process is Due?

In 1884 the court decided "due process" didn't require states to respect the rules for a fair trial listed in the Bill of Rights.

What did due process require?

The court's four attempts over 63 years to answer that question were grandly eloquent but so vague as to be useless. Instead, the court engaged in an 80-year process of deciding on a case-by-case, right-by-right basis which rights the states had to respect.

The 1884 case from California specifically freed the states from the Fifth Amendment requirement to indict capital offenders through a grand jury. In 1900, lawyers for a Utah defendant who had been convicted by an eight-man jury argued that the federal requirement of 12-member juries was part of "due process" and should apply to states. The court said no.

In 1908, a New Jersey defendant asked that the privilege against self-incrimination be applied to the states. Nope, that's not part of due process either, said the court. In 1922, the court ruled that the First Amendment guarantee of free speech applied only to the federal government. "The Constitution of the United States imposes upon the states no obligation to confer upon those within their jurisdiction . . . the right of free speech," the court decided.

Wait. It does eventually get better. Just three years later, the court would take back that statement. But if we freeze the action at this juncture the picture is bleak. It might seem the court could find no meaning in the 14th Amendment at all.

Not so. In an amazing double-twist backflip, the court found the due process clause very handy for striking down state laws that attempted to regulate business or improve the working conditions of laborers.

Corporations Have Rights

The clause, just to refresh your memory, says that no state shall "deprive any person of life, liberty or property without due process of law." The key words for this portion of the story are "person" and "property." In 1886, the court decided corporations were "persons" under the 14th Amendment. Corporate property is protected by due process. When applied to corporate property or the liberty to make anti-labor contracts, the court found great meaning in due process.

The Fifth Amendment says a person must be fairly compensated if his property is taken by the government. In an 1897 case of a railroad that felt it was treated unfairly by the city of Chicago, the court found that the right to fair compensation was a basic part of due process, so states and cities had to respect it.

New York tried to limit the workweek of bakers, for health reasons, to no more than 10 hours a day or 60 hours a week. In 1905, the court used the due process clause to strike down that law, saying it violated the freedom of contract. Kansas tried to outlaw so-called yellow-dog labor contracts, in which workers have to promise, as a condition of their employment, never to join a union. The court struck down the law and upheld such contracts. State efforts to regulate railroad or utility rates, establish a minimum wage or improve working conditions met the same fate.

It Gets Better

In 1925, the court considered the case of Benjamin Gitlow, a New York Communist who had been convicted of criminal anarchy for speeches and publications asserting that organized government should be overthrown by force.

Gitlow had indeed advocated revolution and "the annihilation of the bourgeois parliamentary state." But, his lawyers argued, such statements created no real danger of violent criminal acts. They asked the Supreme Court to throw out Gitlow's conviction and declare the New York law an unconstitutional violation of freedom of speech and press.

The Supreme Court didn't liberate Gitlow. But in its decision, Justice Edward T. Sanford wrote: "Freedom of speech and of the press . . . are among the fundamental personal rights and liberties protected by the due process clause of the 14th Amendment from impairment by the states."

Although it did Gitlow no good (he was later pardoned), the court had finally found an individual liberty tucked somewhere between "due" and "process."

In 1931, the court used the same reasoning to free a defendant and strike down two state laws — a press censorship law in Minnesota and a California law against publicly displaying a red flag. The incorporation of the Bill of Rights within the due process clause was on.

The general doctrine by which most of the Bill of Rights has been applied to the states is called "selective incorporation" — "incorporation" because the rights are held to be incorporated within the due process clause, "selective" because the court retained the option of deciding which rights were in and which were not.

In 1932, the court overturned the convictions of several black youths in Alabama who had been convicted and sentenced to death for allegedly raping white women. They didn't have lawyers until the day of the trial. The court found that the Sixth Amendment guarantee of effective legal assistance at trial, at least in a capital case, had snuck into the due process clause as well.

Curiously, the court that made these breakthrough civil liberties decisions in the 1930's was the same court that was so conservative in its rejection of New Deal economic programs that it provoked President Franklin D. Roosevelt's famous and unsuccessful court-packing plan.

Incorporation continued in 1934, when the freedom of religion clause was applied to the states. In 1937, in another anti-communist case, freedom of assembly was incorporated.

Momentum Lost

But also in 1937, the court stopped the momentum of incorporation. In a Connecticut case, it refused to help a defendant who had been tried twice for the same crime, an apparent violation of the Fifth Amendment prohibition against double jeopardy.

In that case, Justice Benjamin Cardozo wrote that the court had meant what it said all along: The 14th Amendment did not apply the whole Bill of Rights to the states, only the most fundamental rights. Freedom from double jeopardy didn't qualify.

In the next 24 years, only one important incorporation occurred — a 1947 decision applying the First Amendment prohibition against an establishment of religion to states and public schools.

If we stop the action in 1960, this was the status of Americans' civil liberties:

All First Amendment freedoms of expression — religion, speech, press and assembly — had been converted during the 1930's into guarantees against government abridgement at either the state or federal level. But of the free trial rights enumerated in the Bill of Rights, only one — the right to have a lawyer at your trial, and then only if you faced the death penalty — had been incorporated.

In 1961, the heyday of the Earl Warren court, the most liberal in our history, the dam broke.

That year, the right to be free in your home from unreasonable searches and seizures was applied to the states. And the exclusionary rule was applied, meaning that evidence seized during an improper search couldn't be used. Also in 1961, the constitutional prohibition against cruel and unusual punishment was applied to the states.

In 1963, in the famous Gideon case, the court extended the right to have a lawyer, even if the court has to appoint one at public expense, in all felony cases. In 1964, the court reversed its 1908 precedent and declared that the Fifth Amendment privilege not to be compelled to testify against yourself applied to the states.

In 1967 the court ruled that due process required states to provide a speedy trial and to allow a defendant to subpoena witnesses in his own behalf. In 1968, the court overturned a Louisiana conviction and ruled that all criminal defendants have a right to a jury trial. That's right, until 1968 the Constitution permitted a state to deprive a defendant of a jury trial.

In 1969, the last major incorporation was made. It overruled the 1937 decision on double jeopardy and applied that right — the right not be tried twice for the same crime — to the states.

In 1969, Chief Justice Warren was replaced by Warren Burger. The Burger court narrowed some of the earlier incorporation decisions but did not incorporate any additional rights.

A SHORT CONSTITUTIONAL

What is the "due process" that the 14th Amendment requires the states to respect?

Between 1884 and 1947, four different justices tried to answer that question with general descriptions. In each case, the language is so vague as to be useless in communicating what procedures the 14th Amendment required.

Here are the four statements:

1884. Justice Stanley Matthews said the due process clause requires the states to respect "those fundamental principles of liberty and justice which lie at the base of all our civil and political institutions." In that decision, the court found that the right to have your case considered by a grand jury before being tried for a capital offense did not to "lie at the base of all our civil and political institutions." The defendant, who had killed his wife's lover, died in jail while waiting to be hanged.

1908. Justice William Moody wrote that in deciding whether a right was included within due process, the court would apply this test: "Is it a fundamental principle of liberty and justice which inheres in the very idea of a free government and is the inalienable right of a citizen of such a government?" In that case that court ruled the privilege of a defendant not to testify against himself didn't meet the test. The defendant

was ordered to serve his term of six years at hard labor for bank fraud.

1937. Justice Benjamin Cardozo took another stab at defining the test. Is the right "of the very essence of a scheme of ordered liberty?" Other lesser rights may be mentioned in the Bill of Rights, Cardozo wrote, but they could be abolished "and justice still be done." The defendant had been convicted of second-degree murder, which didn't carry the death penalty, then retried for the same crime and convicted of first-degree murder. Cardozo and the court majority ruled that the right not to be tried twice for the same crime was one of those that could be abolished. The defendant died in the electric chair.

1947. Justice Felix Frankfurter wrote that the due process rights that applied to the states were only "those canons of decency and fairness which express the notions of justice of English-speaking people even to those charged with the most heinous offenses." This was another self-incrimination case. The defendant, convicted of murder, died in the gas chamber.

Part Three:
LEFT OUT OF
THE CONSTITUTION

19

Indians: A Trail of Tears

"Great nations, like great men, should keep their word," Supreme Court Justice Hugo Black wrote in his 1960 opinion of a lawsuit between the Tuscarora Indian Nation and the Federal Power Commission.

Black's sentiment reflects what we like to believe is one of the great blessings of the U.S. Constitution. It makes us a nation of laws and of honor. The subtle and intricate wisdom of the great charter throws a protective blanket of rights and liberties, principles and morality over all Americans.

The Constitution gives treaties the status of "supreme law of the land." Black was talking about such a treaty, between the United States and the Tuscaroras, when he said a nation should keep its word. He felt the United States had given its word that the Tuscarora Nation could live on its reservation forever.

But Black was in the minority in that case. The majority voted to let the Federal Power Commission take, with compensation but against the tribe's wishes, more than one-fifth of the Tuscarora reservation in upstate New York for a big hydroelectric power project.

The Fifth Amendment authorizes the federal government to take a person's land, if due process is observed and just compensation is paid. The Tuscarora nation, in the 1960 case, asked for special treatment for its land, based on its treaty rights and its special relationship to the land.

The desire of many tribes to be treated as separate nations is vexing to many Americans — when we bother to think about it at all. We think of the United States as one nation, indivisible, from sea to shining sea. We are proud of our record of absorbing members of diverse ethnic and religious groups who came voluntarily (except the African slaves) to our shores seeking freedom and economic opportunity.

Why don't these Indians get with the program? Don't they know there's milk and honey on this side of the cultural barrier?

But Indian tribes aren't like other groups. And they have often claimed that their special legal status gives them a right not to be treated like other groups. After all, the land we live on was their land.

The Cherokee Tragedy

Two cases in the 1830's involving the Cherokee Nation laid the foundation for what has become the puzzle of constitutional law for Indians. The Cherokees lost one and won one in the courtroom. But what happened to them outside the courtroom constitutes a shocking stain on the honor of our nation.

The Cherokee Nation made treaties with the U.S. government in 1785 and 1791 assuring the Cherokees' right to live in a big chunk of Northwestern Georgia, land they had occupied since before Columbus came.

Over the next few decades, the Cherokees prospered as few tribes ever have, and adopted many of the trappings of white American civilization. The Cherokees had schools, newspapers and Christian churches. They farmed the land plantation style (including the use of black slaves), adopted a written Constitution and declared themselves a sovereign nation.

White Georgians wanted the land, all the more so when gold was discovered there. In the early 1820's, Presidents James Monroe and John Quincy Adams insisted that the treaties be honored. Andrew Jackson, a veteran Indian fighter, was elected president in 1828 partly on a pledge to move the Indians west.

Emboldened by Jackson's support, the Georgia Legislature in 1828 claimed the Cherokee territory and made it a crime for Georgians to obey Cherokee law. The Cherokees sued, arguing that the state law violated their treaty. While the case was pending, Georgia authorities upped the stakes by hauling a Cherokee leader named Corn Tassell out of Indian territory and sentencing him to hang for murder.

The Supreme Court ordered Georgia to delay the hanging until the court ruled. Georgia hung him anyway. That's right — the state defied the U.S. Supreme Court and got away with it. Then the Supreme Court dismissed the Cherokee case in 1831, stating that it had no power to decide the case.

"The Indians are acknowledged to have an unquestionable and heretofore unquestioned right to the lands they occupy," Chief

Justice John Marshall wrote, suggesting that if he could decide the case, he would decide in favor of the Cherokees. But the Constitution gives the Supreme Court jurisdiction over suits brought by foreign nations. The Cherokees claimed to be a foreign nation, but Marshall decided they weren't exactly that.

What were they, then? "They may, more correctly, perhaps, be denominated domestic dependent nations," Marshall wrote. "Their relation to the United States resembles that of a ward to his guardian." In this case, the guardian threw its ward to the wolves.

The issue resurfaced in 1832, but this time the plaintiff was an American citizen. The Rev. Samuel Worcester was a Congregationalist missionary preaching among the Cherokees. Worcester was abducted from Indian country and convicted of breaking a Georgia law prohibiting whites from living in Cherokee territory without a state license. He was sentenced to four years at hard labor.

His appeal, based on the argument that Georgia had no authority over Cherokee territory, reached the Supreme Court without having to pass any test about the status of the tribe. This time, Marshall tipped the court majority to a decision in favor of Cherokee sovereignty.

"The Cherokee nation is a distinct community occupying its own territory," Marshall wrote in 1832, "in which the laws of Georgia can have no force, and which the citizens of Georgia have no right to enter, but with the assent of the Cherokees themselves, or in conformity with treaties and with the acts of Congress. The whole intercourse between the United States and this nation is, by our constitution and laws, vested in the government of the United States."

He ordered Georgia to release the minister.

Despite its murkiness, Marshall's theory of the legal status of tribes has persisted ever since. Tribes are not foreign nations, although they have some aspects of sovereignty. They outrank the state governments in some ways, but are subject to acts of Congress. The U.S. government has some sort of legal-moral obligation to treat them kindly because they are weak and dependent.

The story has a sad and shocking ending. For the second time in two years, Georgia told the U.S. Supreme Court to stuff it. Georgia defied the court again, refusing to release Worcester — and got away with it again.

"Now Let Him Enforce It"

President Jackson, according to legend, remarked: "John Marshall has made his decision, now let him enforce it if he can." Although the authenticity of the quote is in doubt, Jackson refused to use presidential power to enforce the order.

The supreme law of the land, as interpreted by the supreme court of the land, was on the Cherokees' side, but it did them no good because sometimes we are a nation of power, not of laws. Neither the Cherokees nor the Supreme Court had the political or military power to enforce the law of the land.

The Jackson administration then negotiated in 1835 a treaty with an unrepresentative splinter faction of the Cherokee, in which the Indians agreed to vacate their land in exchange for money plus land west of the Mississippi (in what would later become Oklahoma).

The great majority of Cherokees, who had denounced the treaty and unsuccessfully petitioned Congress not to ratify it, refused to leave.

In the spring of 1838, 7,000 U.S. soldiers began dragging Indians to stockades. In the chaos that ensued, some families were divided, never to be reunited. One rebellious Indian was executed, and the soldiers forced his fellow Cherokee to form the firing squad. As fast as any portion of the Cherokee Nation could be cleared of Cherokees, white settlers charged in and either took over the buildings or burned them down.

That winter, the troops forcibly marched 14,000 Cherokees west. Some walked. Some rode horses or wagons. Severe weather and short provisions took their toll. About one-fourth died along the way of disease and exposure. The path they traveled has come to be known as "the Trail of Tears."

A SHORT CONSTITUTIONAL

The U.S. Constitution mentions Indians twice. "Indians not taxed" don't count in the apportionment of seats in the House of Representatives. And Congress is authorized "to regulate commerce with foreign nations, and among the several states, and with the Indian tribes."

From these clues, Congress, the executive branch and the courts have puzzled out the legal status of the tribes. Are they sovereign nations? Can they govern their own affairs? Does a state have authority over an Indian reservation? Are Indians U.S. citizens? Do they have constitutional rights?

The answers given to all of these questions over the years have been a resounding "yes and no."

A few of the basic principles of constitutional law affecting Indians are as follows:

Who Has Sovereignty?

Indian tribes are nations, but not foreign nations. The U.S. government made more than 600 treaties with the tribes. In 1871, Congress declared an end to new Indian treaties. By then, all tribes were established on reservations.

Indian nations have special sovereignty rights over their reservations. The courts have held that tribal governments in some ways are equal to the governments of the states.

One-Way Treaties?

The tribes' special sovereignty stops at the door of Congress. Its power over Indian commerce has grown into "plenary power," which means Congress can do anything it wants with Indian land, including break the treaties.

Tribal rights under most of the 600 treaties were simply overwhelmed by the westward expansion of Euro-Americans or were violated by acts of Congress.

But in a 1903 decision, the U.S. Supreme Court said Congress can violate Indian treaties. In that case, three tribes had a treaty with the United States guaranteeing that their reservations couldn't be sold or broken up without the written consent of three-fourths of the adult males.

Congress passed a law breaking up the reservation without the necessary three-fourths consent. The tribes sued.

The Supreme Court ruled that Congress' plenary power includes the right to disregard the treaties when the national interest requires it. What kind of a treaty is it that only one party has to honor? Hmm. Good question.

Moral Obligation?

Along with plenary power, the federal government developed the "trust doctrine," which said that because the tribes were weak and dependent, the more powerful federal government must look out for their welfare. This humanitarian-sounding principle is cited in vague, moralistic and often highly racist and ethnocentric terms in many key court decisions.

"As a superior and civilized nation, (the United States has) the power and the duty of exercising a fostering care and protection over all dependent Indian communities," one decision says. Another urges the United States to behave as "a Christian people in their treatment of an ignorant and dependent race."

The exact obligation of the United States under this doctrine is never spelled out. The "trust doctrine" is all the more ethically confusing because it is often cited to justify federal actions tribes oppose.

Wavering on Reservations

Congress has wavered in its commitment to the reservation system. Treaties guaranteed the reservations for all time. But in 1887, Congress empowered the president to break up reservations and allot the land to individual Indians. The goal was "inducing the Indian to forsake his wandering habits and adopt those of a civilized life."

The policy was a disaster. Over the next 90 years, about two-thirds of all Indian lands passed from Indian control. In 1934, a new policy, based on preservation of the reservations and respect for the tribe's limited sovereignty, was adopted. In 1953, Congress reversed itself again, stating that the goal of Indian policy should be to terminate the reservation system, discontinue special benefits and legal status for tribes, and bring Indians into the cultural and economic mainstream. This policy was officially repudiated in 1970.

Over the last two decades, Indian treaty rights over land, water and fishing have been upheld. Recognition of the special sovereignty of tribes — subject to Congress' plenary power — has come into fashion.

Indians U.S. Citizens?

The Constitutional language excluding "Indians not taxed" from representation in Congress meant most Indians were not citizens. And non-citizens had no constitutional rights.

The 14th Amendment, ratified in 1868, said: "All persons born or naturalized in the United States and subject to the jurisdiction thereof, are citizens of the United States." The 15th Amendment, ratified in 1870, gave all citizens, regardless of race, the right to vote.

But in 1884, the Supreme Court ruled that an Indian living in Omaha who had renounced his tribal allegiance and was subject to taxation still wasn't a citizen and couldn't vote (although he could become a citizen if he went through naturalization proceedings).

In 1924, Congress extended citizenship to all Indians. An Indian living off the reservation is entitled to full protection under the Constitution. On a reservation, the issue is complicated by the fuzzy doctrine of limited tribal sovereignty.

In 1968, the Indian Civil Rights Act gave defendants, even in tribal courts, most protections of the federal Bill of Rights. But in 1978, the Supreme Court said federal courts couldn't enforce those rights. In practice, the Constitution still doesn't apply on reservations — at least not to Indian defendants — unless the tribal courts choose to apply it.

20

Blacks: From Plessy to Brown

One of the most famous and one of the most infamous of U.S. Supreme Court decisions, 58 years apart, treated the same constitutional question and came to opposite answers.

The question was racial segregation. More specifically, does the U.S. Constitution's 14th Amendment guarantee of "equal protection of the laws" outlaw segregation? In 1896, in the case of Plessy vs. Ferguson, the Supreme Court said by a vote of 7-1 that a Louisiana law requiring separate railroad cars for whites and blacks was constitutional, as long as both races had equal facilities. The separate-but-equal doctrine threw a cloak of constitutional respectability around six decades of unbridled discrimination against black Americans.

What about the degradation of being relegated to a separate car, separate bathroom, separate school? In 1896, Plessy's lawyer had argued that such official insults imposed legal inferiority on blacks. The court went into what you might call its Martian routine to answer the argument. When the court finds the social and political conditions of the real world inconvenient, it can pretend it has just flown in from Mars and knows nothing of earthling reality.

The law requiring separate rail cars for whites and blacks doesn't say that white cars will be nicer, doesn't say that one race imposes this separation on the other, doesn't mention that anyone should feel degraded. The court said it couldn't understand "the assumption that the enforced separation of the two races stamps the colored race with a badge of inferiority. If this be so, it is not by reason of anything found in the act, but solely because the colored race chooses to put that construction on it."

In 1954 the Supreme Court came down from Mars. In Brown vs. the Board of Education, the court unanimously ruled that "in the field of public education, the doctrine of separate but equal has no place. Separate educational facilities are inherently unequal." The Brown decision relied not only on laws and briefs but also on books of psychology and sociology. "To separate (black children) from others of similar age and qualifications solely because of their race generates a feeling of inferiority as to their status in the community that may affect their hearts and minds in a way unlikely ever to be undone," Chief Justice Earl Warren wrote.

The Brown decision represents one of those historic moments when the Constitution approached our most heroic image of it — the nine justices rising as one, taking the side of the underdog, declaring racial equality as the law of the land no matter the consequences.

But the history of the legal status of black Americans before Brown makes one wonder why blacks bothered to seek protection under the Constitution. For the the first century and two-thirds of constitutional history, the document gave the nation's highest legal sanction first to the enslavement and later to the official degradation of blacks.

From 1787 to 1865 the Constitution was the slaveholder's friend. Blacks, even those who weren't slaves, had "no rights which the white man was bound to respect," according to the 1857 Dred Scott decision.

The 13th Amendment abolished slavery in 1865. The 14th Amendment made blacks citizens in 1868. The 15th Amendment enfranchised them in 1870.

It is easy to assume that the Jim Crow segregation laws simply picked up where slavery left off. Not so. During the 1870's and '80's, Southern blacks voted, held office and enjoyed most citizenship rights. Not until the 1890's had racist regimes re-established control over many Southern states, backed by the terror of the Ku Klux Klan. Laws reducing blacks to second-class citizenship, stripping them of their votes by poll taxes, literacy tests and grandfather clauses, mostly date from that decade forward. When the Supreme Court declared segregation constitutional in 1896, it was not just going with the flow, it was taking sides in the struggle to re-enslave blacks when the outcome of that struggle was still in doubt.

The Great Dissenter

Justice John Marshall Harlan, the one dissenter from the Plessy decision, made clear that Plessy was a turning point and that a broader meaning of equal protection was known in the 1890's. In a spirited dissenting opinion, which coined the phrase that "our

Constitution is color-blind," Harlan predicted that the Plessy decision would invite brutal aggressions against rights of black citizens and would encourage the states to "defeat the beneficent purposes which the people of the United States had in view when they adopted the recent amendments of the Constitution."

Harlan, a native of Kentucky and himself a slaveowner before the Civil War, did not agree with the majority's statement that segregation contained only an imaginary, self-imposed insult to blacks. "Everyone knows that the statute in question had its origin in the purpose, not so much to exclude white persons from railroad cars occupied by blacks" but to keep blacks out of the white cars, Harlan wrote. "No one could be so wanting in candor as to assert the contrary." But Harlan's brethren were exactly that wanting in candor. Separate-but-equal became the law of the land. States competed to find the cleverest ways to subjugate blacks.

Separate But Equal

The "equal" part of the doctrine was a sad, cruel joke. In a 1917 survey of 11 Southern states, spending per pupil for white schools was about four times higher than for black schools.

The "separate" part was enforced by the law of the land and by the lynch mob. Lest we fall into the easy assumption that the problem was limited to the South, in 1920 a mob broke into the Duluth, Minn. jail and lynched three blacks held on suspicion of raping a white woman.

Here is a sampling, compiled by Richard Kluger in his book "Simple Justice," of some of the "Jim Crow" laws that held blacks in second-class status. All the laws were in effect in 1951:

Texas prohibited interracial boxing matches. Florida prohibited white and black students from using the same textbooks. In Arkansas, a black couldn't walk into a polling place in the company of a white. In Alabama, a white nurse couldn't treat a black patient. Six states said white and black prisoners couldn't be chained together. In eight states, parks, playgrounds, bathing, fishing and boating facilities, amusement parks, racetracks, pool halls, circuses, theaters and public halls were segregated by law. Eleven states required blacks to ride in the back of the bus. And, in 1951, 17 states and the District of Columbia required segregated public schools. Four more states permitted the practice on a local option basis. That's 21 of the then-48 states. Legalized school segregation was not limited to the deep South.

The Road to Brown

Because the 1954 Brown decision is so famous, we tend to view it as a bolt from the blue. Actually it was the climax of a long series of cases in the 1930's, '40's and early '50's, led by lawyers for the National Association for the Advancement of Colored People (NAACP). The cases stripped the fig leaf of credibility from the separate-but-equal doctrine.

In the 1930's, Missouri operated a law school for whites but none for blacks — separation with no pretense of equality. An aspiring black law student sued and in 1938 the Supreme Court ordered Missouri to either build a law school for blacks or let the black man into the white school.

In the 1940's, Texas tried to head off the Missouri precedent by opening a black law school, but the faculty, library and other facilities were so blatantly inferior to those at the white law school that the Supreme Court, still operating under separate but equal, ordered Texas to provide a truly equal legal education for blacks, or admit blacks to the white school.

The University of Oklahoma tried another approach. It admitted black applicant George McLaurin to the graduate program in education, but required him to sit in a "coloreds only" section in all of his classes, to study at a segregated table in the university library and to eat at a segregated table in the cafeteria. In 1950, the Supreme Court ordered Oklahoma to stop humiliating McLaurin. But the decision carefully avoided overturning the Plessy precedent. It left open the option that a state could solve the problem by providing schools that would be separate but truly equal.

The NAACP was winning its cases, but as long as Plessy remained the guiding principle, segregated schools would be treated case by case. The court would decide whether separate-but-equal schools were being maintained.

The Brown case came from Kansas. Partly to deflect tension in the South, that case became the shorthand name for the ultimate school desegregation case, but it represents five cases from Virginia, South Carolina, Delaware, Kansas and the District of Columbia. Arguing the five cases jointly before the Supreme Court, the NAACP urged the court to acknowledge that separate schools could never be equal. Even if facilities and budgets could be equalized, it argued, black children were stigmatized by the knowledge that the state considered them unfit to go to school with whites.

Oral arguments in the cases were heard in Washington in December of 1952. The justices discussed the case that month. Notes from the conference suggest that four justices were ready to throw out the Plessy doctrine. One was determined to stand by it. Four took no clear position and seemed interested in some middle ground or some delaying tactic. The court under Chief Justice Fred Vinson was badly fractured. Most of the justices agreed that on such an explosive issue they should try to reach a unanimous decision. But Vinson couldn't bring it off. The court agreed to stall, ordering the lawyers to reargue the case in late 1953. Before the rehearing occurred, Vinson dropped dead of a heart attack.

Justice Felix Frankfurter, who felt that the court desperately needed new leadership for the segregation cases, remarked to a former clerk that Vinson's sudden death was "the first indication I have ever had that there is a God."

Politics and the Court

President Dwight D. Eisenhower, in his first year in office, made a highly political appointment.

Gov. Earl Warren of California had never been a judge. He had been Thomas Dewey's running mate on the losing GOP ticket in 1948, and had been a dark-horse candidate against Eisenhower for the Republican nomination in 1952. Warren was sworn in as chief justice in October of 1953, just two months before the rehearing on the segregation cases. When the justices began their deliberations in December, Warren made clear he would vote to reject the doctrine of separate but equal, guaranteeing a majority for that position. To unify the court, Warren needed a decision that clearly and firmly rejected separate-but-equal to satisfy the hard-line liberals on the court, but that would avoid a tone of scolding the states that practiced segregation, so that the Southerners on the court, even the justice most devoted to Plessy, might sign it.

We like to think of the Supreme Court as above politics, but Warren needed all his skills as a politician to get everyone on board. It took five months. Warren read the decision from the bench May 17, 1954.

"Does segregation of children in public schools solely on the basis of race . . . deprive the children of the minority group of equal educational opportunities?" Warren asked. "We believe it does."

The Brown decision didn't end racism, nor segregation in the United States. Both are still with us. In fact, the court has placed close limits on the extent to which the Constitution can be used against *de facto* segregation. But the Brown decision did remove the blessing of the Constitution from *de jure* segregation.

A SHORT CONSTITUTIONAL

Two members of the current U.S. Supreme Court played roles in the historic school desegregation decision Brown vs. the Board of Education.

Thurgood Marshall was the chief lawyer and strategist for the National Association for the Advancement of Colored People. He argued many cases before the Supreme Court and coordinated the team of lawyers and social scientists that finally convinced the court to overrule the doctrine of separate but equal.

In 1967, President Lyndon B. Johnson appointed Marshall as the first black Supreme Court justice.

William H. Rehnquist, the current chief justice, was a law clerk to Justice Robert Jackson when the court first heard the Brown case. Rehnquist wrote a memo arguing in favor of continuing the separate-but-equal doctrine.

The memo plagued Rehnquist during his confirmation hearings when he was appointed to the court by President Richard Nixon and again in 1986 when he was elevated to chief by President Reagan. He has insisted that he was writing what he understood to be Jackson's position, although no other evidence suggests Jackson ever leaned toward reaffirming the constitutionality of segregated schools.

21

Women: Almost Equal Rights

The year was 1961. Three states allowed no women jurors. Eighteen others made it harder for women to get on juries or allowed them to be excused just because of their gender.

Florida's law said any man (except the aged, infirm or those with special occupational conflicts) would automatically be on the list of potential jurors, but for a woman to get on the list, she had to volunteer. In one Florida county the 10,000 names on the jury roll included only 10 women. A woman, convicted of murder by an all-male jury, appealed. The gender bias in the Florida system made her trial unfair, she claimed.

The most liberal Supreme Court in U.S. history, led by Chief Justice Earl Warren, heard the appeal. The Warren Court had decided in 1954 that the "equal protection" clause of the U.S. Constitution prohibited racially segregated schools. Now the question was, did "equal protection" mean men and women must have an equal opportunity to be jurors?

Think you have this one figured out? Hold onto your expectations.

The court upheld the Florida system, and the woman's conviction.

Why? As the court explained without a dissenting opinion, a "woman is still regarded as the center of home and family life. We cannot say that it is constitutionally impermissible for a state, acting in pursuit of the general welfare, to conclude that a woman should be relieved of the civic duty of jury service unless she herself determines that such service is consistent with her own special responsibilities." The Law of the Land still held that a woman's place was in the home.

The 1961 decision was consistent with previous rulings on the constitutional status of women. For most of its history, our Constitution, which we like to think of as a guarantor of legal equality, guaranteed inequality between men and women.

Not until 1971 did the Supreme Court strike down a law that discriminated against women. It has struck down several more since then, and Congress has outlawed the most common kinds of sex discrimination, such as paying a man and a woman differently for the same work. But even now the Supreme Court holds that gender discrimination is more constitutionally acceptable than racial discrimination.

No Women Need Apply

The Constitutional Convention of 1787 was a men's club, yet the original Constitution made no reference to gender. It didn't have to. The idea that a woman could vote, hold office, sit on a jury or own property without a man's guardianship was foreign to the mind of the time. The male bias was so firmly established that no one challenged it in court for 86 years.

In 1873 an Illinois woman who had been denied a license to practice law because of her gender finally raised the challenge. The Supreme Court sided with Illinois, holding that God wanted it that way.

"Man is, or should be, woman's protector and defender," Justice Joseph Bradley wrote in his concurring opinion. "The paramount destiny and mission of woman are to fulfill the noble and benign offices of wife and mother. This is the law of the Creator."

In 1868, the 14th Amendment added "equal protection" to the charter, but that language aimed only at racial discrimination. The Supreme Court made that clear in 1880. While striking down a West Virginia law that banned blacks from jury service, the court volunteered its opinion, though the issue was not raised by the case, that a state "may confine the selection (of jurors) to males."

In 1920, after a long campaign, the ratification of the 19th Amendment secured voting rights for women. But voting was the only right affected.

During World War II, with millions of men off fighting, unprecedented numbers of women took jobs outside the home. But when the soldiers returned, traditional gender roles were enthusiastically restored. The Supreme Court confirmed the trend in 1948 when it considered a Michigan law that banned women, except the wife or daughter of the bar owner, from serving drinks.

The court acknowledged "vast changes in the social and legal position of women." But it said: "The Constitution does not require legislatures to reflect sociological insight or shifting social standards ... Michigan evidently believes that the oversight assured through ownership of a bar by a barmaid's husband or father minimizes hazards that may confront a barmaid without such protecting oversight. This Court is certainly not in a position to gainsay such belief." The Michigan law was upheld.

During the 1950's and '60's the Warren court used the 14th Amendment to interpret racial equality and civil liberties into the Constitution, but it did nothing about sex discrimination.

Burger Court

The year was 1971. An Idaho law said that if a man and woman with equal claims and qualifications sought to be executors of an estate, the probate court should give the job to the man.

An Idaho woman, deprived of the chance to administer her dead son's estate, challenged the law. Her appeal reached a Supreme Court that had changed most of its personnel since the 1961 decision upholding Florida's discriminatory jury system.

Earl Warren had retired. The social and legal upheavals of the 1960's were history. The first two Nixon appointees, led by Warren Burger, had been added. Two more appointments were pending. "Law and order" and "strict construction" were the judicial slogans of the day.

Idaho defended its discriminatory probate law. It promotes family harmony by heading off a dispute between two relatives seeking control of an estate, the state argued. By arbitrarily picking the male candidate, Idaho added, the state saves the trouble and expense of a hearing to pick one of the contestants.

Those arguments don't wash, the Burger court unanimously ruled. "By providing dissimilar treatment for men and woman who are thus similarly situated, the (Idaho law) violates the Equal Protection Clause," Burger wrote.

The framers of the Constitution must have turned over in their monuments.

Just 184 years after our sacred national charter was written, just 103 years after the equal protection clause was added, the law of the land was interpreted to require a degree of legal equality for women. And it was done when the court was supposedly swinging to the right, flying in the face of easy assumptions about what liberal vs. conservative courts are supposed to do.

What are we to make of this? Had new evidence come to light on the true intent of the framers? Was Earl Warren, for all his apparent progressivism, a secret sexist, and Warren Burger, despite his conservative image, a closet feminist? Or is it possible that, contrary to the 1948 barmaid decision, the Supreme Court, the keeper of the Constitution, *does* sometimes require laws to reflect sociological insights and shifting social standards?

In the 10 years between the two Supreme Court decisions, Betty Friedan had published "The Feminine Mystique" (1963), the breakthrough polemic against sexism sometimes credited with reviving feminism. Congress had passed the Equal Pay Act in 1963 and included gender discrimination in the Civil Rights Act of 1964. The National Organization for Women was formed in 1966. In 1970 the Women's National Strike for Equality had generated mass demonstrations around the nation.

According to myth, the Constitution is beyond the reach of transitory political and social events. Secure in their life-tenured, non-political jobs, the justices of the Supreme Court can give exclusive attention to the enduring spirit of the Constitution, the wisdom of the framers as illuminated by previous Supreme Courts.

In reality, Supreme Court justices, like all living beings, are creatures of their times. They share most of the attitudes of the society around them. They gain their jobs through an intensely political process, nomination by the president and confirmation by the Senate. The process is unlikely to put revolutionaries on the court. If they get too far out of step with the social, political, economic and moral mainstream of their times, the court's legitimacy is called into question. It happened in 1954, when the court's school desegregation order challenged the social system of the South. The decision met with massive resistance in the South. It has happened since the court's 1973 abortion decision.

But it has happened rarely, and it didn't happen with a "liberal" court's sexist decision in 1961, nor with a "conservative" court's feminist decision in 1971. Why? Because both decisions were in sync with the rapidly changing mood of the nation on women's rights.

A SHORT CONSTITUTIONAL

Gender equality under the Constitution remains unsettled. The defeat of the proposed Equal Rights Amendment (ERA) during the 1970's left the U.S. Supreme Court to ponder the degree to which the equal protection clause of the 14th Amendment bans sex discrimination.

Since 1971, the court has struck down some sexist laws and practices and upheld others.

Is there a pattern? The court developed a legal theory to explain and justify its acceptance of certain kinds of discrimination over others. But in practice, the justices left themselves enough elbow room to set legal equality of the sexes at whatever level feels comfortable.

The theory is that the equal protection clause implies a ranking of the different kinds of discrimination. A racially discriminatory law can only be upheld if it is necessary to accomplish a "compelling governmental interest." Such laws will be subjected to "strict scrutiny." Few will survive. By comparison, a law that discriminates between between two types of businesses will get a fleeting judicial glance. If the distinction has a "rational basis," that's good enough.

In 1976, the court invented a third, in-between level of scrutiny, for gender-based discrimination. Sex discrimination can be constitutional, the court decided, but "classifications by gender must serve important governmental objectives and must be substantially related to achievement of those objectives." This standard, often called "intermediate scrutiny," met one of its stiffest tests in 1981. The lawsuit — brought by a young man but supported by the National Organization for Women — challenged the law requiring 18-year-old males, and only males, to register for a standby military draft.

Was this gender discrimination "substantially related" to an "important governmental objective?" National defense preparedness was important. But was the exclusion of women — even with women already performing many noncombat jobs in the military — "substantially related" to that objective? When you try to apply the standard, its mushiness becomes clear. The words can mean almost anything you want them to mean. By a 6-3 decision, the Supreme Court agreed with Congress that the United States was not ready in 1981 to draft women.

22

Japanese-Americans: Justice for All?

Can U.S. citizens be subjected to a race-based curfew, taken from home against their wishes, held behind barbed wire for years though they have done nothing wrong?

We like to believe that such things can't happen under the U.S. Constitution. Even in a time of hysteria, our mythic Constitution is a refuge of calm. Its guarantees of equal protection and due process can withstand even war and panic and race hatred and politics. But, during World War II, those things happened to 112,000 Japanese-Americans. Appeals to the Constitution were denied. Perhaps most disturbing, the Supreme Court delayed ruling on the constitutionality of imprisoning thousands of innocent citizens until it was too late for the ruling to make any difference.

A piece of parchment is always calm, but never courageous. The people who interpret and enforce our sacred national piece of parchment are capable of bravery and wisdom or panic and cowardice. It comes with the animal. In calm times, the keepers of the Constitution have courageously stood up for the freedoms of speech and association, even for those who want to speak about communism and associate with fellow radicals.

But in the 1920's, just after the Bolshevik Revolution, and during the Joe McCarthy period of the 1950's, America was in a tizzy about Communism. The panic showed in Supreme Court decisions. The court upheld the use of loyalty oaths to exclude Commies from the workplace, convictions based on membership in Communist organizations, convictions for speaking and publishing Communist doctrine. In the 1930's and the 1960's, when anti-Communist shrieks subsided to the usual dull roar, the court regained its composure and established an American's right to speak or publish any political doctrine and join any association.

The persecution of Japanese-Americans during World War II, with its ugly barbed-wire evocation of concentration camps, is probably the most galling instance of the Constitution failing to live up to its myth of courage. Edward Ennis, a Justice Department lawyer during the 1940's whose job required him to defend the Japanese internment, which he privately opposed, later called it "the greatest deprivation of civil liberties by government in this country since slavery."

Pearl Harbor

After the sneak attack on Pearl Harbor in 1941, many Americans assumed that the Japanese would assault the West Coast, where most Japanese-Americans lived. Rumors abounded that Japanese-Americans planned sabotage or espionage missions. Residents of coastal areas reported strange lights flashing from the coast, which they took to be Japanese-American traitors signaling to enemy ships. No such reports were substantiated.

Fear and panic breathed life into the xenophobia that always lurks beneath the surface. Famous liberals, such as the columnist Walter Lippmann and Earl Warren, then attorney general of California, joined the call to get the Japanese off the coast.

President Franklin D. Roosevelt issued the executive order that made it possible. Congress lent its authority by making it a crime to disobey military curfew or evacuation orders.

Gen. John L. DeWitt, commander of the West Coast defenses and a man whose motto was "a Jap's a Jap," issued the detailed orders. First, he imposed a curfew that applied only to ethnic Japanese. Then he ordered all Japanese on the coast to report for evacuation. The orders granted a few days to dispose of homes and businesses, allowed evacuees to take only as much as they could carry, and provided for their internment for an unstated period in camps from California to Arkansas. Those interned suffered losses estimated at between $3.4 billion and $4.2 billion, according to a recent brief arguing for restitution.

Evacuation happened quickly. Few internees resisted. FDR signed the order in February of 1942. The first curfew took effect March 24. On March 30, the first few thousand were ordered to report for "relocation," as the euphemism called it. On June 7, the last order was issued. The number of internees finally peaked at 111,999.

The orders made no distinction between citizens and aliens. In fact, about 70,000 U.S. citizens were imprisoned. Most disturbing to a sense of constitutional fairness, the relocation program made no effort to distinguish those whose behavior had raised some question about their loyalty to the United States.

The stereotype of the inscrutable Asian was invoked to justify the policy. The idea was that with an Asian, even one who seemed loyal might be up to something. DeWitt summarized the feeling with his comment that "There isn't such a thing as a loyal Japanese."

Minoru Yasui put his faith in the Constitution. Gordon Hirabayashi did too. They didn't believe that race-based assaults on the rights and liberties of loyal citizens could be consistent with the constitutional guarantees of equal protection and due process. They offered themselves as test cases to find out whether such things could be constitutional.

At 11 p.m on March 29, 1942, just hours after the curfew took effect, Yasui walked into a police station in Portland, Ore., and asked to be arrested as a curfew violator. He was a lawyer and an officer in the U.S. Army Reserve (although when he had offered himself for active duty, he had been rejected).

Six weeks later, Hirabayashi, a senior at the University of Washington, turned himself in at FBI headquarters in Seattle. He declared he was defying the evacuation order.

Fred Korematsu, a California welder, had plastic surgery to conceal his Japanese features, but it didn't work. He was arrested two weeks after Hirabayashi. All three men were convicted. They appealed.

The Court Takes a Stand

The cases reached the Supreme Court in 1943. One year was already gone from the lives of the Japanese-Americans. The court made matters worse by dodging the issue. In the first case, Yasui's appeal, the court upheld the curfew law. But that was no longer relevant, since the curfew had been in force only briefly before evacuation and internment.

The second appellant, Hirabayashi, had violated both the curfew and evacuation orders. But since the trial judge hadn't given him any extra jail time for refusing to be evacuated, the Supreme Court decided it didn't have to decide anything about the evacuation.

The third appellant, Korematsu, had violated the evacuation order, but the court bucked the case back to the lower courts on a procedural issue. All three decisions were unanimous, but they didn't start out that way.

Justice Frank Murphy, a strong civil libertarian, drafted a blistering dissent, historian Peter Irons wrote in "Justice at War," his study of the Japanese internment cases. Murphy noted that the government had not offered any evidence that Japanese-Americans were generally disloyal, nor had it made any effort to separate disloyal from loyal citizens so they could be treated accordingly. "Instead of this, by a gigantic round-up no less than 70,000 American citizens are placed under a special ban and deprived of their liberty because of a particular racial inheritance. . . . This is so utterly inconsistent with our ideals and traditions, and in my judgment so contrary to constitutional sanctions, that I cannot lend my assent. . . ."

The argument that the nation had to do whatever was necessary to win the war had limits, Murphy argued. "We do not win the war, on the contrary we lose it, if we destroy the Constitution and the best traditions of our country." Murphy circulated the draft of his dissent to his brethren on the court. And yet, even as outraged as Murphy was by the internment program, he was persuaded to drop his dissent for the sake of wartime unity.

No Military Reason

By the summer of 1944, U.S. and allied forces were advancing in Europe and Asia. The war would last another year, but victory was in sight. One regiment of Japanese-American soldiers, some of whom were released from internment to fight, had received more than 18,000 decorations for valor. The American leadership knew that Imperial Japan could not threaten the U.S. mainland. The new general in charge of West Coast defense certified that internment could not be justified by any military reason.

But 1944 was an election year, and California was a key state. Roosevelt knew that release of the internees would be controversial, probably unpopular. The Pentagon instructed the West Coast command to make no change in the internment program until after the election.

FDR won a fourth term by a huge margin.

The next month, Fred Korematsu's case, which the Supreme Court had sent back to the lower courts 18 months earlier for clarification of a procedural question, returned to the Supreme Court. It had a new running mate.

Mitsuye Endo had been a 22-year-old clerical worker at the California Department of Motor Vehicles when the war started. American born, raised a Methodist, with a brother serving in the U.S. Army, Endo neither spoke nor read Japanese, had never visited the homeland of her ancestors and had no contact with the old country. In short, she was as American as baseball and apple blossom pie. Nothing in Endo's record cast any doubt on her loyalty. Yet she had been fired from her job, ordered from her home and interned for two and a half years at a converted racetrack near San Francisco.

Unlike Yasui, Hirabayashi and Korematsu, she had not violated the army commands. But, in July of 1942, she challenged the internment program by asking that the government be ordered to give a reason why she should not be released. The other three cases had dealt with curfew and evacuation orders. But since none of the defendants were in internment camps, the Supreme Court had been able to pretend the camps didn't exist. Endo's petition forced them to deal with internment, the most extreme violation of liberties of the batch.

On Dec. 18, 1944, the Supreme Court decided against Korematsu, but in favor of Endo. The four cases, taken together, came out this way:

In wartime, a curfew based on race is constitutionally acceptable. Ordering Americans, on the basis of their race, to evacuate their homes is also acceptable. To hold them in a camp while determining which of them are loyal is also acceptable. But to continue holding them after their loyalty has been certified (as Endo's loyalty had) was not acceptable.

"We are of the opinion that Mitsuye Endo should be given her liberty," Justice William O. Douglas wrote for the court. The decision was handed down Dec. 18, 1944, more than two and a half years late for thousands of Japanese-Americans. It was also one day too late to matter.

With Roosevelt safely re-elected and the war in its final phase, the Army had announced the previous day that all internees (except those subject to individual internment orders based on some evidence of disloyalty) would be released.

A SHORT CONSTITUTIONAL

After years of neglect, the World War II internment of Japanese-Americans has been back in the news in recent years. Here are some of the latest developments as of October of 1987:

Nov. 12, 1986: Retired attorney Minoru Yasui, 70, died of cancer in Denver. The first to challenge the Japanese curfew law, he had spent a year in solitary confinement and never was cleared of his criminal record.

June 1, 1987: Japanese-American plaintiffs, seeking billions of dollars restitution from the federal government for losses caused by their internment, suffered a setback when their case, which had reached the Supreme Court, was sent back to a lower court on technical procedural grounds. The Justice Department, while conceding that the internment was "deplorable," opposed the suit, arguing that the statute of limitations expired.

Sept. 17, 1987: The U.S. House of Representatives approved a bill that would apologize for the internment and pay each surviving internee $20,000. The bill is pending in the Senate. The Reagan administration opposes it.

Sept. 24, 1987: A federal appeals court overturned the 45-year-old conviction of Gordon Hirabayashi, the second person to resist the curfew law. The court concluded that the curfew was based on racial, rather than military, reasons. Hirabayashi, 69, is a retired sociology professor, now living in Edmonton, Alberta. He hopes the U.S. Justice Department will appeal the ruling so he can seek exoneration from the Supreme Court. The Justice Department has not announced whether it will do so.

Part Four:
THE CONSTITUTION IN OUR TIMES

23

Contragate and the Constitution

Was the Iran-Contra mess a constitutional crisis?

The text of the U.S. Constitution says nothing directly about rescuing hostages, selling arms, supporting foreign guerrillas, shredding documents or reimbursing White House aides for business expenses with money laundered through Swiss bank accounts. It makes no mention of the National Security Council. Heck, it doesn't even mention the Cabinet. It doesn't say that a sitting president can don a private-citizen cap and put the arm on the king of Saudi Arabia to donate millions to the Contra rebels fighting to overthrow the government of Nicaragua. And it doesn't say he can't.

But make no mistake about it — Contragate is up to its armpits in the Constitution. The text of the Constitution does have a couple of relevant things to say on the subject, but the Constitution's place in the affair comes more from its non-text roles as magic talisman of the Republic, symbol of virtue, protector of the accused and argument settler of last resort.

Constitution as Text

It's easy to get bogged down in the minutia of Contragate. Did the Boland Amendment, in which Congress banned undercover aid to the Contras, cover the National Security Council? Can the president authorize a covert operation orally, or only in writing? Did Marine Lt. Col. Oliver North send five memos to his boss describing his Contragate activities, as North recalls, or only one, as the boss, former National Security Adviser John Poindexter, recalls? But from a constitutional perspective, the story is not that complicated. The Constitution is clear on these points: Congress is supposed to make the laws. The president and his subordinates are supposed to faithfully execute them: That's why they call it the executive branch.

The Boland Amendment may suffer from ambiguous draftsmanship. But it is clear that Congress was trying to end covert aid to the Contras. The president and his men connived to keep the aid flowing.

Boom. Constitutional crisis.

What about national security? Throwing this phrase around gives a constitutional flavor to the idea that the president can't always play strictly by the rules. But "national security" isn't mentioned in the text of the Constitution. One of the purposes of the Constitution, mentioned in the preamble, is to "provide for the common defense." But the Constitution also gives Congress the sole power to declare war. The last time anyone checked, Congress had not declared war on the Sandinista regime in Nicaragua, nor on Iran, nor on Iraq.

Constitution as Symbol

President Reagan is a master of symbolic uses of America's founding myth. That's one reason he told the American people that the Contras, whom he prefers to call the "Nicaraguan freedom fighters," are the "moral equivalent of our Founding Fathers." In that instance, he didn't make the sale. If he had, Congress wouldn't have dared cut off lethal aid to the Contras.

North allegedly cooked up an even more audacious scheme to plant a constitutional halo on the Contras. According to a story in the *Los Angeles Times,* North plotted to have the Contras adopt the U.S. Constitution as the charter of their government-in-exile. North reportedly wasn't sure whether to have the Contras hold their constitutional convention off the shore of Philadelphia (where George Washington and the boys did it in 1787) or down in Grenada (scene of America's triumph against Marxism).

"Ollie wanted to do it on Grenada for symbolic reasons," said a source who the *Times* said had worked on the project, "but everyone else thought that was too much. It was just too tacky." North used to rub his hands with glee as he contemplated the prospects, the sources said. How, the reasoning went, could U.S. congressmen, who are sworn to protect and defend the Constitution, turn their backs on a campaign to apply our very own Constitution to a nation practically on our borders?

Constitution as Hideout

North's 1985 effort to wrap the Contras in the Constitution stalled, but by December of 1986 he discovered that the charter made an even more suitable cover for his own suddenly vulnerable legal position.

With all the attention North received for the self-avowed candor of his appearance before the Iran-Contra investigating committee in July of 1987, people may have forgotten about the effort the previous December to get him to tell the good, the bad and the ugly about his activities to the House Foreign Affairs Committee.

"I don't think there's another person in America who wants to tell the story as much as I do," he assured the committee members. Poignantly, he reminded them that as a Marine he, too, had sworn to support and defend the Constitution. He had "tried to do so honorably," he said, his chest heavy with medals, his voice trembling with emotion, but now that he stood suspected of crimes, he had to "avail myself of the protections provided by that same Constitution that I have fought to support and defend." In other words, he took the Fifth. He asserted his Fifth Amendment right not to testify on the grounds that it might incriminate him. As did his ex-boss, Poindexter. As did his favorite arms dealer, retired Gen. Richard Secord. As did many of the key players. North almost made it sound as if the Constitution somehow forced him to clam up, and he maintained his silence until he had negotiated a deal that nothing he told the special congressional committee could be used against him.

Some folks got mad at North and Poindexter for putting selfish concerns ahead of the country's need to know what had happened. Some got mad at Reagan, believing that if the commander-in-chief ordered these military men to tell what they knew, they would have to comply or face court-martial. Reagan said he sure wanted the truth to come out, but that he couldn't order folks to give up their constitutional rights.

But nobody got mad at the Fifth Amendment.

The Infallibility of the Constitution

When Mafiosi take the Fifth, when those accused of violent crimes take refuge behind it, and when North and company assert their right not to divulge what they had been doing in the White House, the Fifth Amendment protection doesn't seem like such a hot idea.

But, heck, it's in the Constitution isn't it? It must be good.

Yes, we tell ourselves, the no-compulsory-self-incrimination privilege is inconvenient and frustrating at times, but it is one of the bastions of freedom and justice.

Or is it? Mickey Kaus of the *New Republic* magazine doesn't think so. "What these ritual bows to the Constitution never include is a persuasive justification for the amendment," Kaus wrote. "That is because there is none. True, the amendment once served important purposes," Kaus wrote, such as preventing the torturing of witnesses until they confessed, as had happened under the notorious Star Chamber tribunals in 17th-century England. "But subsequent advances in jurisprudence have rendered it obsolete. All of its original purposes can be, and already are, achieved by other, far less destructive constitutional rules." Repealing the Fifth Amendment privilege would not legalize government torture, nor would it repeal the First Amendment, so the rights of political and religious dissenters would still be protected.

Okay, the arguments for and against the Fifth Amendment privilege deserve a full-fledged debate. But the point is that they seldom get such debate outside of law review articles, because the amendment basks in the reflective glow of our sacred national charter. Suggesting that the Fifth Amendment is an impediment to justice or that the Electoral College is undemocratic brings down the wrath of the minions of the constitutional religion. In a nation with so many legal freedoms of thought and expression, ought it not be possible to discuss whether some provisions of the Constitution have outlived their usefulness?

The System Works

As Contragate wound down, we heard the comforting fadeout music we sing at the end of constitutional crises. We heard it at the end of Watergate and at the end of the Vietnam War, when Sen. Frank Church had exposed some abuses by the Central Intelligence Agency, and back when Sen. Joe McCarthy was censured for excessive Commie-baiting. In this crisis, we started singing it as soon as the Tower Commission had issued the first report.

The system works.

Yes. The republic still stands, the Constitution is still in effect, some of the participants have been forced from public office.

Legislative reforms will be adopted and some semblance of the separation of powers will be restored. Most reassuring of all, we will be able to tell ourselves, the truth came out. These accomplishments should not be taken lightly.

But when we take them as proof that the system works, what are we telling ourselves? Did the Constitution catch the illegal diversion to the Contras of profits from the illegal arms sales to Iran? No. In fact, a member of the special congressional investigating committee suggested that if someone had given the right Swiss bank account number to the sultan of Brunei, the secret Contra funding would not have been discovered.

The argument goes like this: The Contras desperately needed funds to continue their war. North's network tried to oblige. Assistant Secretary of State Elliot Abrams solicited a Contra contribution from the potentate of the little oil-rich nation of Brunei. (Abrams later lied to a congressional committee about the solicitation.) The sultan tried to deposit $10 million in the Swiss account used by the Contras. Because he was given the wrong number, the money went into the account of a Swiss businessman instead. The fumble made the Contras' financial plight more desperate. This desperation led to the scheme to divert profits from the secret Iranian arms deals to the Contras, basically to replace the missing millions. The arms deals were uncovered by a Beirut magazine, picked up by the U.S. press, and we were off to the races.

Was this the system at work? Hardly. Did the system catch the Watergate burglars? No, a private security guard did. Did the system end the Vietnam War? Maybe so, but not until tens of thousands had died.

The Constitution has played a role — and a big one — in allowing the facts of Contragate to come out. The congressional committee is part of the system. The free press, another part of the system, makes it possible for ordinary citizens to learn what their executive branch has been up to. And the system, Fifth Amendment and all, will allow fair and orderly trials for those charged with crimes. But when we tell ourselves at the end of each constitutional crisis that the system solved the problem, we are invoking the myth that nothing can go too far wrong as long as we have the Constitution.

Constitutional crises such as Contragate can be interpreted just the opposite way. They show how far wrong things can go despite the Constitution.

The Constitution is not a self-executing document. The system works when people make it work and fails when people let it fail.

24

At War Against the Constitution

Abraham Lincoln, as a young congressman in the 1840's, wrote to his law partner: "The provision of the Constitution giving the war-making power to Congress was dictated, as I understand it, by the following reasons: Kings had always been involving and impoverishing their people in wars, pretending generally, if not always, that the good of the people was the object. This our (Constitutional) Convention understood to be the most oppressive of all kingly oppressions, and they resolved to so frame the Constitution that no one man should hold the power of bringing oppression upon us."

Let's face it, the guy had a way with words. Furthermore, Lincoln had his facts right. The Constitution, as written, ratified and amended, gives presidents no authority to start wars, enter wars, provoke wars, commit warlike acts or even put troops where they might become involved in hostilities, without advance congressional authorization. But over the two centuries since the framers laid down their quills, their plan has been turned on its head. Every president since World War II has violated the framers' plan by using U.S. troops without advance congressional authorization.

Presidents have tried various legal theories and word games to justify their acts of war. Harry Truman said the Korean War was not a war but a "police action" authorized by the United Nations Charter. President Lyndon Johnson claimed that Congress approved his Vietnam escalation by the Tonkin Gulf Resolution. But he started the escalation before the resolution passed, and President Richard Nixon continued the war after Tonkin was repealed. When Nixon spread the war to Cambodia, it was only an "incursion," he said. President Reagan classified the conquest of Grenada as a "rescue mission" of American medical students. The evidence that the students were in danger was murky at best. But if the goal was rescue, why change the government of Grenada?

Reagan said that was justified by the invitation of Grenada's neighbors, a theory that has nothing to do with congressional authorization or international law.

The word games haven't really fooled anyone. Presidents have gotten away with extra-constitutional war powers largely because of the widely held belief that we are engaged in the biggest, longest and most dangerous undeclared war of all — the Cold War against Communist expansionism.

Congress acknowledged the reversal when it passed the post-Vietnam War Powers Act (over Nixon's veto). The law requires the president to inform Congress after he sends the troops abroad and allows him to continue hostilities for 90 days unless Congress disapproves. Even if fully enforced, the law would not re-establish Congress' constitutional authority to decide in advance whether a war would be just, worthwhile and winnable. Yet, in a stunning Constitution headstand, presidents have denounced the law as an unconstitutional invasion of executive power.

Congress has never declared that U.S. forces were involved in "imminent hostilities." It has never invoked its power under the 90-day rule, and the act has never been tested in court. The War Powers Act has flopped. But even if it worked it would only have confirmed the pre-eminence of the president.

This revision of our Constitution has not occurred by amendment, or even by court interpretation, but by what your major thinkers would call historical imperatives. In other words, nobody believes that the framers' plan is suited to modern realities.

The constitutional division of war powers made sense when potential enemies were a wind-powered ocean voyage away, the argument goes. But it is unworkable for a nuclear superpower with global responsibilities and vital interests everywhere.

In theory, that argument isn't supposed to be good enough. Our Constitution is the law of the land. If it doesn't work, we have to amend it. We can't disregard it just because it seems outmoded.

In practice, we can and sometimes do disregard the Constitution. If presidents, congressmen, federal judges and the American people consider the original war powers clause irrelevant to the modern age, historical arguments don't matter. Original intentions or not, the framers' plan will have to stand or fall on its merits. The conventional wisdom is that it wouldn't work.

The Framers' Plan

The Constitution authorized Congress to declare war. It made the president commander-in-chief. These two clauses are sometimes cited to suggest that the legislative and executive branches were meant to be roughly equal partners in war powers. The suggestion is flat wrong. In addition to the power to declare war, the Constitution goes on explicitly for seven paragraphs to put Congress in charge of preparing for, beginning and controlling all forms of hostility known to the framers.

By contrast, the president's title of commander-in-chief is the only constitutional language that gives him any war powers. This was understood to give him substantial, but not total, control over the military once Congress had authorized hostilities. The only case in which the framers intended the president to engage in hostilities without prior congressional action was to defend against a sudden attack on U.S. territory. Thus the framers' plan would allow the president to respond if our radars picked up incoming missiles.

Not just fear of monarchy, as Lincoln wrote, but love of peace motivated the framers' plan. They didn't mean to ban war, but to make it less likely. They believed a large, deliberative, representative body was less likely to start a war than was an individual. Thomas Jefferson wrote that the framers had "given an effectual check to the dog of war by transferring the power of letting him loose from the Executive to the Legislative body." And they were right. Congress has declared five wars in 200 years of constitutional history. Presidents have initiated more than 100 military adventures without war declarations.

Presidents Washington, Adams, Jefferson, Madison and Monroe conceded that Congress was pre-eminent in war powers. The original plan was alive and well in 1859, when President James Buchanan said: "It will not be denied that the general power to declare war is without limitation and embraces ... every species of hostility, however confined or limited. Without the authority of Congress the President cannot fire a hostile gun in any case except to repel the attack of an enemy." Some presidential transgressions occurred in the late 19th and early 20th centuries, but they were few and small compared with more recent presidential wars.

The Nuclear Age

World War II created the modern world. It started the nuclear age and turned the United States and the Soviet Union into two paranoid giants, each thinking the other is bent on its destruction, each with the power to destroy the world a thousand times over.

New ethics and attitudes have overtaken Americans' thinking about war. It's a dangerous world out there. The other side doesn't play fair. Their meganukes can reach us in minutes. They are bent on world domination. Only America, the arsenal of democracy, can hold back the tide of communism. Many Americans have come to believe that our survival and the cause of world freedom depend on the ability to act with secrecy, speed and single-minded determination. Congress, with its slow, public deliberations and its sensitivity to political shifts, seemed ill-suited to such a world. Constitution or no, the president would have to do it.

Now we have experienced 40 years of the Cold War powers plan and a couple of dozen overt and covert presidential military adventures.

We can't replay history to see what would have happened if the framers' plan had remained in effect. But perhaps it is possible to set aside the conventional wisdom for a moment and reconsider the framers' plan on its merits, and perhaps to suggest that they didn't have such a bad idea after all.

Would the major undeclared wars of our times, Korea and Vietnam, have been fought? Would the nation be better off if they hadn't?

Since we failed in Vietnam, damaged our prestige and spent thousands of lives, it seems easy to argue in retrospect that we would have been better off to have skipped that war.

Korea is less often discussed nowadays. American forces did prevent South Korea from "going Communist," but it has required the presence of U.S. troops over 34 years to sustain an undemocratic, capitalist regime. Has it been worth it? Defenders of the war would say that by showing our resolve, we deterred other Communist aggressions, another historical unknowable.

Dwight Eisenhower and Nixon backed covert coups that replaced left-leaning, elected presidents in Guatemala and Chile. Such secret, sudden operations are the kind that almost certainly couldn't occur under a congressional war powers plan. Did these covert actions enhance U.S. security? Probably so, if you believe that any socialist regime in our hemisphere threatens us. Did they contribute to world democracy and freedom? Probably not, since both nations have been dominated ever since by military regimes among the most brutal in our hemisphere. The series of covert U.S. plots against Castro's Cuba have been unsuccessful and have deepened the hostility in the region. The Iran-Contra mess again has demonstrated the difficulty of sustaining covert wars in a democracy.

The death of more than 200 sleeping U.S. Marines in Lebanon in a 1983 bombing turned that undeclared peacekeeping mission into a disaster. The 1986 air strike against Libya was popular at home and strained several of our alliances. It's hard to say if it reduced terrorism. The invasion of Grenada achieved its goals and was popular. Was it necessary to U.S. security?

In none of those instances did Congress refuse to declare war. Presidents didn't ask. So it's not possible to say which of the presidential wars might have been waged if the framers' plan had been in effect. Presumably several would not have occurred. That was part of the framers' idea.

A SHORT CONSTITUTIONAL

Besides the power to declare war, the U.S. Constitution gives Congress power:

"To raise and support Armies; to provide and maintain a Navy; to make Rules for the Government and Regulation of the land naval Forces;

"To provide for calling forth the Militia to execute the Laws of the Union, suppress Insurrections and repel Invasions;

"To provide for organizing, arming and disciplining the Militia, and for governing such Part of them as may be employed in the Service of the United States.

"To define and punish piracies and felonies committed on the high Seas and Offenses against the Law of Nations;

"To grant Letters of Marque and Reprisal and make Rules concerning Captures on Land and Water." (Letters of marque would authorize hostile actions against the ships of a foreign nation with which the United States was not at all-out war.)

25

The Drive for a New Convention

As if you didn't have enough to worry about, here come two nightmares for the United States, offered by two competing groups. Each comes with a solution. Each group claims history, the Founding Fathers and the U.S. Constitution on its side.

Group A, led by the National Taxpayers Union offers Nightmare No. 1. It features a U.S. economy afflicted with the kind of hyper-hyper-hyper-inflation suffered by Germany in the 1920's when, according to legend, you needed a wheelbarrow to carry enough money to buy a loaf of bread. That economic crisis contributed to the collapse of democracy and the rise of Hitler and the Nazis. With the federal deficit hovering somewhere between $150 billion and $200 billion, it could happen here, the NTU implies, unless the Constitution is amended to require a balanced budget. Since Congress has failed to pass the amendment and seems unable to control spending without one, Group A calls for a new constitutional convention to propose such an amendment.

Our Constitution says that if two-thirds of the states petition for a new convention, Congress must call one. The provision has never been used. Between 1975 and 1983, 32 states adopted such petitions — two short of the number needed to force Congress to act. If the drive fails, the NTU literature suggests, the American way of life is at risk.

Group B, coordinated by Citizens to Protect the Constitution (CPC), says the real threat is that the NTU might succeed. The CPC's literature conjures images of a "runaway convention" taken over by radical ideologues. In its nightmare vision of a convention, abortion, church and state issues and gun control are thrown into the hopper as the power-crazed delegates play I'll-support-your-disgusting-amendment-if-you'll-support-mine. It's like playing Russian roulette with the Constitution, says Group B's brochures. The organization's literature features a list of frightening amendments that might be brought up at a convention, including one backed by a neo-Nazi group to force all Americans not of Western European descent back to their ancestral homelands.

Nazism if we call the convention. Nazism if we don't. What's our poor, beleaguered nation to do?

We might try consulting the wisdom of the Founding Fathers and other demigods of American history for guidance. But we'll quickly find them on both sides of the issue. James Madison, father of the Constitution, once said, "Having witnessed the difficulties and dangers experienced by the first convention ... I would tremble for the results of a second." A decade after the Constitution took effect, on the other hand, Thomas Jefferson wrote that he wished he could amend the Constitution with "an additional article taking from the federal government the power of borrowing," which the NTU treats as an explicit endorsement of its balanced budget amendment campaign.

Honest Abe Lincoln himself, in his first inaugural address, endorsed the calling of a new constitutional convention in hopes of heading off the Civil War: "I will venture to add that to me the convention mode seems preferable (as opposed to waiting for Congress to propose amendments), in that it allows amendments to originate with the people themselves, instead of only permitting them to take or reject propositions originated by others not especially chosen for the purpose ..."

Calling a new convention would be a rejection of the work of the framers, says Group B. How so, replies Group A, when the framers put into the charter the very provision for the calling of a convention?

Each side also has a favorite anecdote from 20th-century constitutional history that supports its view of the wisdom of petitioning for a new convention.

Direct Election of Senators

From 1787 to 1913 U.S. senators were chosen by their state legislatures. This vestige of the framers' anti-democratic tendencies was out of step with the populist and progressive eras early in the 20th century. A constitutional amendment for the direct election of senators gained steam. The U.S. House, accustomed to the rigors of direct democracy, passed the amendment five times. For reasons not too hard to guess, the Senate killed the amendment every time. Finally, the states began petitioning for a new convention to propose an amendment for direct election of senators. In 1912, when the campaign was one state short of the two-thirds required, the Senate finally approved the amendment. It was quickly ratified.

The story works well for the NTU in several respects. It associates the constitutional convention strategy with a progressive, democratic, popular amendment. It shows how hard it is to get Congress to do something perceived as a threat to the self-interest of the club. And it illustrates one of the NTU's favorite points. We don't necessarily want a convention, says the NTU's executive vice president, David Keating. We want a balanced budget amendment. We'd be happy to get one out of Congress. The story of the 1912 amendment suggests (although the CPC disputes this interpretation) that if another state or two would adopt petitions, Congress would probably cave in and pass a balanced budget amendment to avoid a convention.

One Person, One Vote

In 1964, the Supreme Court decided the Constitution required that all state legislative districts be apportioned on the principle of "one man-one vote." No more funny business to deprive blacks in the South or urban voters in the North of representation, the court said. This was about as welcome to malapportioned state legislatures as direct election was to unelected U.S. senators. Legislatures petitioned for a constitutional convention to propose an amendment overturning the Supreme Court ruling. The drive petered out. Several states rescinded their petitions, but not until the campaign came (depending on who's counting) within one petition of forcing a convention.

This story helps the CPC argument by associating the new convention strategy with a regressive, selfish, partly racist movement by state legislators. It rebuts the argument that Congress will pass the desired amendment if enough states petition for a convention. Congress didn't do that in 1965.

The Fear Factor

The argument boils down to the fear factor. Which group's nightmare is scarier and more convincing? The smart money is probably on Group B because it claims the Constitution itself, our sacred national charter, is at risk if a new convention is called.

Linda Rogers-Kingsbury, CPC president, argues that once the

convention assembles, nothing can limit it. The whole system would be "up for grabs," CPC brochures say. The only constitutional convention we've had, the one in 1787, was supposed to recommend a few amendments to the Articles of Confederation. But the convention overran its mandate and proposed an entirely new system.

Forced onto the defensive, the NTU argues that there are plenty of safeguards to ensure a convention limited to one reasonable balanced budget amendment. Since we haven't had a constitutional convention for 200 years, no one can say for sure whether a convention could be limited.

Point/Counterpoint

Here, based on the literature circulated by the National Taxpayers Union and the Citizens to Protect the Constitution and interviews with their representatives, are paraphrases of the opposing arguments for and against the calling of a new constitutional convention:

NTU: The state petitions call for a convention limited to the balanced budget. The U.S. Constitution requires that the convention be called by Congress, so Congress could add its voice by calling for a convention specifically limited to the balanced budget amendment. The American Bar Association, which studied the question in the 1974, concluded that Congress could and should limit the convention to the subject for which it was called.

CPC: The convention, receiving its mandate directly from the people, could ignore any congressional limitations. As for the ABA study, it said Congress could and should pass a convention procedures law. But Congress has not done so. The ABA warned that without such procedures, "we could be courting a constitutional crisis of grave proportions."

NTU: The American people can be trusted not to elect a bunch of nutty radicals as delegates. But even if they did, the amendments proposed by the convention would come back through Congress before they could be referred to the states. If Congress felt the convention had run wild and overstepped the convention call, Congress could refuse to pass the extraneous amendments on.

CPC: For Congress to refuse to pass along amendments would be a major constitutional crisis that would have to be decided by the courts. And since nothing like this has ever happened, we don't even know whether the courts have jurisdiction. Anyway, Congress would be under tremendous political pressure to let the state legislatures consider anything the convention proposed.

NTU: That's the best safeguard of all — the states. Nothing the convention proposed would have any effect unless ratified by three-fourths (that's 38) of the states. The legislatures are petitioning for a balanced budget convention — not a repeal of the Bill of Rights. If a bunch of crazy amendments passed the other safeguards, any 13 state legislatures could stop them.

CPC: In a highly charged political atmosphere, anything might happen. The safeguards you mention might work, but they might not. Why take a risk with our precious constitutional rights and freedoms?

26

The Constitution Under Strain

If it ain't broke, don't fix it. So the saying goes, and so most Americans feel about the U.S. Constitution.

Somehow, the magic incantation that begins "We the People" has steered us the people to 200 years of success and prosperity. We win our wars (except the last one); we pay our debts (except the $160 billion federal deficit) and enjoy the highest standard of living (until recently, when we fell behind half a dozen or so Western European countries).

The stability of our Constitution, the oldest written system in the world, makes us the envy of the world (except that the last five presidencies have ended in death, disgrace, divisiveness or defeat. And Ronald Reagan, the most popular recent president, limps toward the finish line with his credibility badly shaken by the Iran-Contra affair.)

Hmm. What if it *is* broke? Could we see past our adoration of the Constitution long enough to fix it?

One Washington-based bipartisan panel dripping with bigwigs and ex-bigwigs with impressive credentials suggests that the answers to both questions is "yes."

Yes, the structure of our government has become part of the problem, says the Committee on the Constitutional System. We devour our presidents. Congress can't act coherently. Party discipline doesn't exist. One year out of every four, the government governs. The other three are devoted to electioneering. Money and politics chase each other in an endless circle, with no place for the national interest to cut in. Voter turnout is among the lowest of world democracies. And since World War II, power has usually been divided between a Republican president and a Democratic Congress, who disagree on what to do.

Yes, the system can be fixed without major surgery. The committee offers seven suggestions requiring five constitutional amendments. The most fundamental would give representatives four-year terms and senators eight-year terms.

The committee is not exactly a bunch of Commie dupes. Its cochairmen are U.S. Sen. Nancy Landon Kassebaum of Kansas, former Treasury Secretary Douglas Dillon, and Lloyd Cutler, former counsel to President Jimmy Carter. Its board of directors includes a slew of past and present members of Congress and the executive branch, mayors and governors, college presidents, deans and other academic illuminati. But no matter how blue-blooded the committee, when you hear a plan that requires five constitutional amendments, you want to holler, "Hey! Be careful with our Constitution, buddy. You're jiggering with a structure that has survived 200 years without major jiggering."

No Myth

When it comes to the structure of the U.S. government, the Constitution is no myth. A two-house Congress, an independently elected president with veto power, the two-year terms of House members and six years for senators were indeed the 200-year-old design of James Madison and the boys. The system has been remarkably stable — no coups, only one civil war and a high degree of public satisfaction.

True, we must constantly reassess our governmental policies. Frequently we must throw last year's idiots out of office and install a whole new set. But that's the beauty of the system. The two parties provide choices. The people rule through ballots, not bullets.

Peter Schauffler, coordinator of the committee, acknowledges that suggestions for constitutional change meet automatic resistance from the it-ain't-broke-don't-fix-it school. Problems exist, Schauffler said, but people blame the individuals running the system instead of considering whether the system needs change.

In a pamphlet proposing its seven-point plan, the committee asserts: "Our public officials are no less competent, either individually or as a group, than they used to be." Here are the committee's diagnosis of the system's ills and its recommended cures:

Signs of Strain

Every member of Congress agrees that the deficit is too high. Reagan rode budget-balancing rhetoric to office. Yet the deficit quadrupled during the Reagan years. A system in which everyone agrees on the goal but no one can move toward it has too many checks and balances, the committee argues.

Since World War II, more than 40 treaties submitted to the Senate have been rejected or died without a vote, the most famous being SALT II, negotiated by the Carter administration. Such a record casts an image of indecision and unreliability.

The president's party has controlled Congress only four of the last 19 years. This syndrome of "divided government" was unusual before World War II but has now become the norm. The committee says it guarantees confrontation and deadlock.

Election campaigns are so long they bore the public, and so expensive you must be wealthy or become dependent on well-heeled special interests to succeed.

In the old days, candidates were chosen by the leaders of their parties, ran on a party platform and relied on the party for campaign funds and workers. The rise of the primary system, modern technology such as television and jet planes, and modern campaign methods such as direct-mail fund-raising have enabled politicians to get elected without the help of the central party organization.

In 1986, 96 percent of members of Congress who sought reelection were successful regardless of how their party fared nationally. Once in office they are less willing to follow the party line from congressional leaders or a president from their own party. Recent incumbents such as ex-House Speaker Thomas P. (Tip) O'Neill Jr. complain that the problem is not lack of leadership but a decline in followership.

Most voters used to vote straight party tickets, often handing in a preprinted straight-ticket ballot distributed by the party. In the election of 1900, 96 percent of congressional districts were carried by a presidential and congressional candidate from the same party. In 1984, because of ticket splitting, this happened in only 56 percent of congressional districts. Ticket-splitting contributes to the likelihood of divided government.

A restoration of party loyalty could counteract some of the centrifugal tendencies of the constitutional separation of powers, the Committee on the Constitutional System argues.

Suggested Changes

The committee endorsed these proposals:
1. *Permit members of Congress to serve in the Cabinet.*

It would encourage cooperation between the legislative and executive branches. The Constitution prohibits this, so an amendment would be necessary.

2. One federal election every four years.

That's one reason to change House terms to four years and Senate terms to eight, requiring two more amendments. Midterm elections almost always mean loss of seats in Congress for the president's party, making the second half of presidential terms less productive than the first. Members of Congress could keep their minds on business longer without worrying about the next election and would need campaign contributions half as often, reducing their reliance on special interest groups.

3. Reduce the requirement for ratifying treaties.

Instead of two-thirds of the Senate to ratify a treaty, make it a majority of both houses. This would require a fourth constitutional amendment.

4. Limit campaign expenditures.

Congressional candidates in the 1986 midterm elections spent $342 million, up 30 percent from the 1982 election. The Supreme Court has ruled that a limit on campaign expenditures violates the First Amendment. To reduce candidates' dependence on moneyed contributors, the committee suggests another constitutional amendment to overturn that decision.

5. Members of Congress as delegates.

The political parties should seat all House and Senate nominees plus holdover senators as uncommitted delegates at presidential nominating conventions. This would guarantee them a voice in the selection of the nominee and increase cohesion between the president and Congress.

6. Public financing of congressional campaigns.

Congress should channel public funds through the parties to congressional candidates for campaign broadcasts. The catch would be that the party and the candidates agree to spend no other funds on broadcasts. This would hold down campaign spending and tie the candidates closer to the party.

7. Optional straight-ticket balloting.

Nineteen states allow voters to vote a straight party ticket by checking one line on the ballot or pulling one lever. This discourages the ticket-splitting that the committee says contributes to the breakdown of party loyalty. The committee suggests that Congress require all states to offer such an option to voters, while still permitting optional ticket-splitting.

27

The Right to be Left Alone

In 1965, Connecticut had on its books an 1879 law that, by the admission of even its judicial defenders, was "uncommonly silly," "obviously unenforceable" and probably "asinine." The law made it a crime for anyone — even a married couple — to practice any form of birth control. A doctor or pharmacist who prescribed, sold or counseled a couple in the use of contraceptive devices was an accessory to this crime, punishable by up to a year in prison. But when the U.S. Supreme Court struck the law down, it started what has become the hottest constitutional battle of our times.

Privacy. Do we have a constitutional right to it? If so, where does it come from and how far does it go? If that doesn't sound like the hottest constitutional question you've heard lately, be fore-warned: "privacy" is polite shorthand for sex, birth control, abortion and sodomy. The three biggest privacy cases so far have gone like this:

■ In the 1965 case (Griswold vs. Connecticut), the court discovered a general right to privacy in the Constitution that placed "the sacred precincts of marital bedrooms" beyond the reach of government.

■ In 1973 (Roe vs. Wade) the court ruled that the right of privacy included the right to have an abortion.

■ In 1986 the court upheld Georgia's sodomy law, ruling that the right to privacy did not extend to the right of homosexuals to engage in consensual sex acts in their own homes.

Welcome to the cutting edge of constitutional liberties and watch out that you don't get cut. At a time when moral and family issues are on the political front burner, we have naturally sought guidance from the myth that binds us. But the framers left us no advice on the subject of bedroom liberties. And the Supreme Court, rather than settling the question, has undermined several of the major myths that keep the system going. Yet the myths stand, perhaps believed as widely as ever, a tribute to their awesome durability.

Endangered Myth No. 1: The Documentary Constitution

No, that doesn't mean the documentary Constitution doesn't exist. It's there in Washington, under glass. The myth is that decisions made in the name of the Constitution bear some clear and close relationship to the words in the document. None but the strictest, strict constructionist or original intentist would demand that every court decision be clearly spelled out in the document. But the myth works best when the latest interpretation appears solidly connected to the parchment.

The word "privacy" is not mentioned in the Constitution. The sudden judicial discovery of such a previously invisible right, 178 years into the mission, is the kind of thing that threatens the myth of the document, unless some credible connection to the parchment can be suggested. But what did the 1965 court come up with?

Even the seven members who voted for it couldn't agree on the source of the right of privacy. The majority opinion by Justice William O. Douglas said privacy was located in the "penumbras" of the Bill of Rights, formed by "emanations" from the guarantees explicitly contained in the amendments. (A penumbra is the light outer edge around the darker center of a shadow, especially one formed by a heavenly body. An emanation is something that flows out of something else.)

. Three justices suggested in a concurring opinion written by Justice Arthur Goldberg that privacy was one of the rights covered by the Ninth Amendment, which says that the people retain all the rights they haven't given away. Goldberg's argument has not been ridiculed as Douglas' has because Goldberg didn't rely on astronomical terms such as "penumbra," but his argument is one of those that turns history on its head. The Ninth and Tenth Amendments were written almost entirely to reassure the states' rights oriented Anti-federalists that the new federal government would not overrun their rights and powers. Yet Goldberg used it to justify a federal court's decision to overrule a state legislature. The historical argument aside, if the Ninth Amendment functions as a blank check to the Supreme Court to fill in new rights, their judicial discretion is unlimited. If the right of privacy can suddenly emerge from the Ninth Amendment, what might pop out next?

Endangered Myth No. 2: Judges Judge, Legislatures Legislate

The myth here is that because it is the least democratic branch, the power of the judiciary is closely limited. Congress and the state legislatures, being the elected representatives of we, the people, should make the detailed decisions about what the law shall be.

Federal judges aren't elected and can't make laws. Their job is to interpret and defend the Constitution that we, the people, adopted 200 years ago. The court can say "no" to legislation that violates the broad, fundamental principles laid out in the great charter, but the myth works best if the judges appear to avoid actually making laws. Thus, in the Roe decision, if the court had decided that the Texas law against abortions violated Jane Roe's constitutional right to privacy, it would have been consistent with the myth that judges do not legislate. But the court didn't stop there. It laid out the trimester plan. A woman can freely choose an abortion during the first three months of pregnancy, the court said. During the second trimester, a state can regulate but not prohibit abortions. During the final trimester, a state can outlaw abortions except those necessary for the mother's health. Even if you believe a constitutional right to privacy exists, and you believe that this right extends to reproductive freedom of choice, it's hard to believe that the concept can be expanded into the complex trimester plan without the judges doing a lot more legislating than is consistent with Myth No. 2.

Endangered Myth No. 3: Consistency

In his majority opinion in the Georgia sodomy case, Justice Byron White seemed to acknowledge the problems the court had created for itself with myths Nos. 1 and 2.

"The Court is most vulnerable and comes nearest to illegitimacy when it deals with judge-made constitutional law having little or no cognizable roots in the language or design of the Constitution," White wrote.

Vulnerable to what? The justices have lifetime appointments. Their decisions cannot be overruled except by themselves or by constitutional amendment. One way of interpreting White's statement is that if the court violates too many of the myths about what it is and how it works, it begins to undermine the beliefs that cause people to accept the court's opinions as the final word. So

White, writing for a bare five-member majority, put a stop to the advancing line of judge-made, unrooted privacy rights. The Constitution guarantees no right of homosexual sodomy. But this was hard to reconcile with the two earlier cases. White said the earlier cases suggested some unwritten constitutional rights on issues that affected marriage, family and pregnancy issues, but that none of those had anything to do with homosexuals.

In an unusually bitter dissent, Justice Harry Blackmun, who had written the majority opinion in the Roe case, accused the court of fuzzing the issue. The question is not whether homosexuals have a constitutional right to engage in oral or anal sex, Blackmun wrote. The question is whether the Constitution guarantees to all Americans "the right to be left alone." If the logic of the earlier cases applies, Georgia has no more business regulating private, consensual acts in the bedroom of its citizens than Connecticut does prohibiting the use of birth control.

By backing away from the logic of its recent precedents, the court thus undermined another myth: that the court will proceed logically and consistently.

Endangered Myth No. 4: Fairness

The Constitution and the court are supposed to be fair and unbiased. Even members of the most despised groups are entitled to the equal protection of the laws. But the Georgia sodomy decision bumped against that myth, too, by suggesting that it might be permissible to apply a law differently against homosexuals. The Georgia sodomy law makes acts of oral or anal sex, whether by homosexuals or heterosexuals, punishable by up to 20 years in prison. But this case concerned a homosexual. The Supreme Court took pains to declare that it upheld the Georgia law only as its applied to homosexual sodomy. In his dissent, Justice John Paul Stevens focused on the unfairness of applying the law only against practitioners of a minority lifestyle.

The fallout from the sex and privacy cases has endangered other myths that help the court and the Constitution maintain their legitimacy.

The system works best when the court can bring the Constitution into line with widely shared mores and ethics of contemporary Americans. But Americans are deeply divided on the issues of abortion and homosexual rights (especially in the AIDS era). In cases where groups disagree strongly, whatever the court decides is bound to be criticized and scrutinized. Criticism and scrutiny can be hazardous to the health of myths.

If the court must deviate from its own precedents, it helps if the precedents are quite old, so the court doesn't appear to be flip-flopping. But the constitutional right of sexual privacy was invented in 1965, expanded in 1973 and retrenched in 1986. Two justices participated in all three cases.

The court appears most legitimate when it appears least political. But the privacy cases — especially the abortion decision — have forced the political aspects of the system into full view. Ever since the Roe decision, groups on both sides of the highly emotional issue have taken a strong interest in the abortion views of Supreme Court nominees. As a candidate, Ronald Reagan all but promised to appoint justices who shared his anti-abortion philosophy. Certainly he was true to his promise when he nominated Robert Bork to a 1987 vacancy on the court. Bork had publicly doubted the existence of a constitutional right to privacy and has criticized the Roe decision.

Supporters of the right to choose an abortion were prominent within the lobbying coalition that defeated the Bork nomination. Such a battle is rough on the myth of the non-political court.

28

The Myth of Original Intent

In the fall of 1987, the nomination of Judge Robert Bork to the U.S. Supreme Court became the most hotly contested Supreme Court nomination of modern times. It ended with Bork's rejection by 58-42 on Oct. 23. But before it was dead, the Bork nomination put some zip into the perpetual controversy over how to interpret the Constitution.

Should the court be bound by the original intentions of the framers of the Constitution and its amendments, as Bork, Attorney General Edwin Meese and President Reagan argued? Or can the justices give modernized meanings to certain words and phrases, while preserving some overall spirit of the document? It may sound like an argument only a law professor could get excited about. But the question affects life-and-death decisions, gets to the root of democracy in America, messes dangerously with the legitimacy of the system and finally settles on the border between constitutional myth and reality.

One of the most appealing myths of our Constitution is that the 200-year-old wisdom of the greatest figures from U.S. history can guide us through our own frightening and confusing times, populated as they are by mere mortals.

The Constitution is full of noble phrases like "cruel and unusual punishment," "necessary and proper," "freedom of speech" and so on. Noble, yes, but vague. The power of the Supreme Court to give the operative interpretation of such phrases is the power to control the laws that bind us.

If any five justices can twist the law of the land into whatever shape they choose, then instead of democracy we have a superlegislature of unelected, life-tenured dictators. So judges must be bound by something other than their own whims, prejudices and preferences. If not the original intent of the framers, what should that be?

Supreme Court Justice William Brennan, in a 1985 speech

disputing Meese's "original intent" campaign, settled on the concept of "human dignity" as the guiding light. For example, capital punishment is inconsistent with human dignity and therefore violates the Eighth Amendment ban on "cruel and unusual punishment," Brennan said. He promised to vote against every death sentence that comes before him.

But the death penalty was common in 1791, when the Eighth Amendment was ratified. The Constitution refers to capital punishment. The citizens of many states, acting through their elected legislatures, continue to want some murderers executed. But Brennan, if he can find four more votes among his brethren, would simply cut it down, using the Constitution as his sword and "human dignity" as his cry. Who elected him to overrule not only the intent of the framers but also the intent of today's voters and legislators? the original intentists ask.

They argue that those, like Brennan, who claim to be bound by things like the evolving spirit of the document, the changing needs of the nation or some code of moral philosophy are not really bound by anything except their *own* moral philosophy and their own sense of what the spirit of the document should be. The original intent of the framers must be the lodestar or the system loses its democratic legitimacy, Meese and Bork have argued. And they are absolutely right. The only trouble is, that the original intent of the framers sometimes doesn't exist, sometimes can't be found and sometimes, when it exists and can be found, is totally unacceptable to modern values.

Whose Intent?

The original Constitution was drafted by 55 unelected delegates, none of whom supported every word in it. It was ratified by special conventions in 13 states attended by more than 1,000 men, many of whom voted against ratification. Those delegates were chosen in special elections. So whose intent are we after, the writers, the ratifiers, or those who voted for those who ratified it? And if those elections gave the original document *its* democratic legitimacy, what are we to make of the 85 percent of the 1787 population — mostly women, blacks and the unpropertied — who had no right to vote?

The amendments to the Constitution, especially the Bill of Rights and the 14th Amendment bring a whole new cast of writers, ratifiers and possibly relevant intentions into the picture. The theory of original intentism suggests that one clear intent existed and was shared by everyone connected with the writing and ratifying of the language. Such is seldom the case.

How Do You Find Intent?

Let's focus on the 55 framers. How do we know what they intended? Intentists often cite the Federalist Papers as if they are a direct expression of the intentions behind the words. The Federalist Papers were essentially sales documents written during the New York ratification campaign. The essays were intended to sway votes for ratification, not to make public the innermost thinking of the Philadelphia framers. The papers were written by James Madison, Alexander Hamilton and John Jay.

Jay, the smallest contributor, was not a delegate to the Philadelphia convention. Hamilton was a delegate, but skipped much of the convention after it became clear that his intentions were far from the mainstream. What weight can we give to Hamilton's Federalist essays, in which he pretends to endorse the perfection of every constitutional provision?

Madison was present every day of the Philadelphia convention and favored most — though certainly not all — of the provisions adopted. One idea for which Madison fought hard at the Philadelphia convention was the creation of a "Council of Revision," composed of the president and the Supreme Court, that would have veto power over all federal and state laws. Unlike the current system in which the courts can only consider a law that is raised in a lawsuit, Madison's plan would have subjected all laws to judicial review before they took effect. And while the courts can strike down only those laws that offend the Constitution, Madison wanted to give the judges power to veto any law they considered unwise.

Original intentists claim Madison on their side when they argue for "judicial restraint," the doctrine that judges should seldom substitute their judgment for that of elected legislatures. Yet Madison's Council of Revision idea makes him a raving judicial activist by the standards of today or any day.

The 14th Amendment added "equal protection" to the Constitution and obligated the states to provide "due process." Most of 20th-century constitutional law has flowed from interpretations of those phrases. Yet the amendment was ratified under duress by the former Confederate states after they were told they would not be restored to full statehood until they ratified. How are we to interpret the intent of the ratifiers of the "equal protection" language if their primary intent was to get the Union troops out of their states?

Did the Framers Intend Original Intentism?

Not even the most ardent original intentists have found evidence that the framers wanted people to pore over their Philadelphia debates, their private lives and letters or their published writings for clues to the true meaning of the Constitution. On the contrary, although disputes about the correct interpretation of the Constitution arose while the members of the convention were still alive, they never published an official journal of the convention. Madison, who kept the best notes during the convention, didn't allow them to be published until after his death, by which time the Constitution was 53 years old.

What Does Original Intentism Yield?

Original intentism can turn ugly on you, as Bork found during his confirmation hearings. The framers were 18th-century men. Some of their ideas, attitudes and actions cannot be given serious weight in the 1980's. For example, take George Mason and the slave's ear.

Since Mason was the Philadelphia convention's strongest advocate for a bill of rights, judges might examine Mason's life for clues to the proper historical meaning of the Eighth Amendment ban on "cruel and unusual punishment." Back home on his Virginia plantation, Mason once had a slave nailed by his ear to a post for several days to punish him for running away. Shocking as this is, Mason was not particularly sadistic. In 18th-century Virginia, such punishment of a runaway slave was not considered cruel and unusual treatment.

When Meese and Bork argue that the court has strayed from the original intent of the Constitution, they focus on decisions that are not universally popular, such as the abortion and affirmative action rulings. They are on solid historical ground when they argue that the framers of the Bill of Rights weren't thinking about the right of women to have an abortion during the first trimester of a pregnancy.

But they tend to favor original intentism only when it advances their own policy agenda. If they followed original intentism all the way, here are some of the well-established constitutional doctrines they would probably have to oppose:

■ Desegregation: The 1866 Senate that put "equal protection" into the Constitution segregated its own gallery by race, making it hard to argue that it intended to ban legalized segregation.

■ Women's rights: The same framers of the 14th Amendment intended no change in the status of women as second-class citizens.

■ Freedom to criticize the government: Seditious libel, meaning criticism of the government that brought the president or the Congress into disrepute, was a common-law crime in the 1780's. When the First Amendment was written in 1789 it was not intended to overturn such laws.

■ One person, one vote: The framers never empowered the federal government to tell the states how to apportion legislative and congressional districts.

So where does this leave us? Original intentism doesn't work, can't work, and if it did work we wouldn't like it very much. But if the unelected Supreme Court appears to be dreaming up the meaning of the Constitution, the system's democratic legitimacy goes kaput. Before you panic, bear in mind that the system has survived this dilemma for decades.

The dilemma is solved if one deals separately with appearance and reality. The Supreme Court must appear to be taking original intent seriously, while in reality it is changing the Constitution to reflect modern attitudes.

And so the court does. Often the decisions that are most inconsistent with original intent are the ones that strain hardest to cite historical evidence. In 1954 the court called the lawyers back for a second round of oral arguments on the original intent of the framers of the "equal protection" clause. They were looking for historical evidence to justify the landmark *Brown* decision ordering school desegregation. In 1964, when the court applied the historically unintended doctrine of one person, one vote to congressional districts, Justice Hugo Black jumped through historical hoops to claim Madison on his side. Furthermore, he had to be aware of how he was mishandling history, because it was pointed out in the dissenting opinion in the case. In the 1965 case that invented the constitutional right of privacy, Justice Arthur Goldberg's concurring opinion quoted heavily from Madison and lightly from Hamilton to justify the ruling on historical evidence.

So when all the shouting's done, do we have a superlegislature of democratically illegitimate life-tenured judges who can do anything they want with the Constitution? Not quite. The justices are at least limited by the need to make a credible historical argument when they want to deviate from historical reality. Otherwise, they might break the spell of belief in the myth of original intentism that legitimizes their authority. The myth that binds us binds them too.

Conclusion

The Soviet Union has a constitution.

It guarantees democratic elections and a republican form of government. Soviet citizens have — on paper — most of the same constitutional rights and liberties as Americans, such as freedom of expression and religion, plus several more that our Constitution doesn't mention, such as the right to a job, to housing and to an education. The Soviet Constitution mandates a foreign policy based on peaceful coexistence and respect for the sovereignty of other nations. Ours gives no such guidance. So you might have to say that they have a better constitution.

On paper that is. In practice, during most of Soviet constitutional history, a Russian who criticized his government as strongly as Jesse Jackson or even Walter Mondale criticizes ours would have found himself taking a vacation in Siberia.

We have a Constitution; they have a Constitution. Ours says freedom; theirs says freedom. Yet we believe that somehow ours produces real freedom and theirs doesn't. How can we explain two such different societies with such similar constitutions? This book has been a search for the source of the magical power of our Constitution to provide and protect the freedom, democracy, equality and justice that we hold so dear.

Perhaps because we have the oldest working written Constitution in the world, we think that just having one is the secret. But many countries, not only the Soviet Union but many of our noncommunist allies, have constitutions that don't provide what Americans would recognize as freedom.

The Framers

Sometimes we attribute our Constitution's greatness to the men who wrote it. We tell ourselves that the framers were wise, selfless men of superhuman foresight who, 200 years ago, saved the nation from the twin demons of anarchy and tyranny and set it on an irresistible trajectory to freedom, democracy, equality and justice for all.

The history of the framing and the framers gets in the way of this appealing and familiar fairy tale. By 20th century standards, the framers were hopelessly racist, sexist and elitist. They devised a system to preserve the special influence of their class. They were interested in liberty, but they gave priority to property rights. When we attribute egalitarian instincts to the framers, we are on the shakiest historical ground of all. They were interested in protecting social and economic *in*equalities.

Such a view seems hard on the framers. It is also unfair. Blaming a bunch of rich, white 17th century males for being out of step with 20th century attitudes about freedom, democracy and equality is as absurd as asking them to anticipate laser beams or genetic engineering. Trying to turn them into 20th century men also blinds us to the framers' real contributions. We understand and appreciate them better if we view them in the context of their own times.

The key difference between the George Washington-James Madison group and Patrick Henry's faction was the question of nationalism. The framers were men of vision, but their vision was of a nation, united by a strong central government. The nationalists were brilliant tacticians who schemed tirelessly to promote "the plan," as they often called the Constitution. And they pulled it off. They created a national government able to raise taxes and raise armies, regulate commerce and rationalize the money supply, conquer and settle the vast Western lands, turn the 13 states into 50, and generate unprecedented prosperity.

The framers were in their graves by the time the Civil War finally sealed their victory, establishing once and for all the supremacy of federal over state power. If we like the way the nation has turned out, we have plenty to thank the framers for. But civil liberties, democracy and equality were not among their top priorities.

Amendments

The framers left us a document that could be amended, although with great difficulty. The 26 amendments have increased the democratic, libertarian and egalitarian content of the Constitution. But long after the Bill of Rights was adopted, Massachusetts had a state religion, Southern states banned anti-slavery speeches and books, and states sometimes deprived criminal defendants of fair trial rights. Even after the 14th Amendment suggested that states observe the Bill of Rights, the Constitution didn't prevent the states from abridging those rights. We can't conclude that amendments have made us free.

The 14th Amendment also promised "equal protection of the laws." But long after that phrase became the Law of the Land, blacks, women and Indians were second-class citizens. Amendments did not banish inequalities from the system.

Democracy has received many boosts by amendment, but amendments cannot make us a democracy. In the framers' time, about 15 percent of the population was eligible to vote. About 75 percent of Americans can now vote. Yet the voter participation percentage in the 1986 federal election dropped to 37 percent of those eligible.

The Supreme Court

Is it the Supreme Court, then, that has made the Constitution a guarantor of freedom, democracy, equality and justice for all? The court has played a key role in determining the libertarian, egalitarian and democratic content of the system. The court's power to *interpret* gives it the power to *change* the meaning of the Constitution from the original intentions of its authors. Otherwise, we would be stuck with the outmoded, often unacceptable attitudes of the dead. But if we acknowledge the court's power too openly, we undermine our pretenses of governing ourselves through elected representatives.

The court's power comes from public acceptance of its legitimacy. But its legitimacy depends on maintaining the appearance that the court is bound by precedent and original intentions. So the justices must make a credible claim that they are interpreting within those original intentions. Sometimes the claim is more credible, sometimes less so. But we help the court by our general desire to believe that the game is being played according to the rules.

Even under this arrangement, the court is not always the guarantor of constitutional liberty and justice. Sometimes the court uses its power to back away from those goals. As recently as World War II, the court found constitutional rationales to deprive Japanese-Americans of due process and the presumption of innocence.

We the People

Where else can we look for the magic of the Constitution if not to the document, the framers, the amendments or the Supreme Court? This book has suggested we should look to ourselves.

By calling the Constitution "The Myth that Binds Us," I haven't meant that the Constitution is a lie. A myth is not a lie. A myth is a story that may or may not be consistent with history but that gains its power from people's belief in it. The Constitution's power over us is the flip side of our power over it. It becomes what we believe it is, and we become what we believe it makes us.

How does it work? As silly as this might sound, it works sort of like the Wizard of Oz.

Remember the climactic scene when Dorothy, the Scarecrow, the Tin Man and the Cowardly Lion meet the wizard in his great hall in the Emerald City? They find a giant, green disembodied face floating in the air declaring that it is the great and powerful Wizard of Oz. But then Toto, the little dog, pulls back a curtain in the corner of the room and exposes a pudgy little man, turning wheels, pushing buttons and speaking into a microphone. The face in the air bellows: "Pay no attention to the little man behind the curtain." But they can see the little man saying into the microphone: "pay no attention to the little man behind the curtain."

When we pull back the curtain on the myth of the Constitution, the authors, amenders, ratifiers and interpreters of the Constitution turn out to be mere mortals, like the wizard and like ourselves. At first, the realization seems to rob the wizard of his magic powers. How can a mere mortal give the scarecrow a brain, the tin man a heart or the lion courage? How can a mere man-made document make us free?

But remember what happens next in the movie. The wizard tells the scarecrow that he has a brain if only he believes he has one. And the scarecrow suddenly starts spouting Pythagorean theorems.

The Constitution can't make us a democracy — not if it's just a document written by men long dead and interpreted by mere mortals of today. But if we believe it makes us a democracy, and we act like a democracy, then we are a democracy. If we believe it makes us respect one another's basic liberties, then we have our liberties. If we believe the Law of the Land requires us to treat each other as legal equals, we try to obey.

The Myth that Binds Us

Sure, there's a document called the Constitution. That's no myth. It's in Washington, under glass, if you want to visit it. But the Constitution that binds us is the one we have in our heads. That mythic Constitution performs functions no 200-year-old parchment ever could.

It functions as the bible of our national civic religion. Created by demigods through the "miracle at Philadelphia," it gives us the word on how to run a government and a society. It is interpreted by its own special order of black-robed priests who pore over the text seeking an ever-higher understanding of its true meaning. We have faith that the answers to our most troubling national questions lurk somewhere within the writ. And so we find it there.

The Constitution is also a history book. Every generation adds a chapter, leaving a record of the political, economic, social and moral trends of its time.

It's also a mirror in which we can see our own aspirations. What kind of nation are we trying to be? A nation of freedom, democracy, equality and justice? We look into the constitutional mirror and see those aspirations promised and almost — but never quite — within our grasp.

Finally, the Constitution is a medium through which each generation translates itself into the Law of the Land.

The responsibility for the Constitution is ours now. George Washington, James Madison and Patrick Henry laid down the burden long ago. We have the opportunity to make the Constitution more of a guarantor of freedom, democracy, equality and justice. If we fail, we have no one to blame but we, the people of the United States of America.

Bibliography

Beard, Charles A., *An Economic Interpretation of the Constitution of the United States,* (Free Press, 1986).

Benedict, Michael L., *The Impeachment and Trial of Andrew Johnson,* (Norton, 1973).

Bowen, Catherine Drinker, *The Miracle at Philadelphia,* (Little, Brown, 1966).

Collier, Peter , *When Shall They Rest? The Cherokees' Long Struggle With America,* (Holt, Rinehart & Winston, 1973).

Congressional Quarterly, *Guide to the U.S. Supreme Court,* (Congr. Quarterly, 1979).

Cortner, Richard C. *The Supreme Court and the Second Bill of Rights,* (University of Wisconsin Press, 1981).

Curtis, Michael K., *No State Shall Abridge,* (Duke University Press, 1986).

Deloria, Vine and Lytle, Clifford M., *American Indians, American Justice,* (University of Texas Press, 1983).

Dewey, Donald O., *Marshall versus Jefferson: The Political Background of Marbury v. Madison,* (Knopf, 1970).

Farrand, Max, *The Records of the Federal Convention of 1787,* (Yale University Press, 1911).

Fehrenbacher, Don E., *The Dred Scott Case,* (Oxford U. Press, 1978).

Finkelman, Paul, *An Imperfect Union: Slavery Federalism and Comity,* (University of North Carolina Press, 1981).

Irons, Peter, *Justice at War,* (Oxford University Press, 1983).

Johansen, Bruce E., *Forgotten Founders, Benjamin Franklin, the Iroquois and the Rationale for American Revolution,* (Harvard Common Press, 1982).

Kelly, Alfred and Harbison, Winfred, *The American Constitution,* 5th Ed., (Norton, 1982)..

Kluger, Richard, *Simple Justice,* (Knopf, 1976).

Levy, Leonard W., *The Establishment Clause, Religion and the First Amendment,* (MacMillan, 1986).

Levy, Leonard W., editor, *Freedom of Press from Zenger to Jefferson,* (Bobbs-Merrill, 1966).

MacLeod, Duncan J., *Slavery, Race and the American Revolution,* (Cambridge University Press, 1974).

Mayer, Henry, *A Son of Thunder,* (F. Watts, 1986).

McDonald, Forrest, *E Pluribus Unum,* (Liberty Press, 1979).

Miller, Charles A., *The Supreme Court and the Uses of History,* (Belknap Press, 1969).

Morris, Richard B., *Witnesses at the Creation, Hamilton, Madison, Jay and the American Constitution,* (Holt, Rinehart & Winston, 1985).

Smith, Page, *The Shaping of America,* (McGraw-Hill, 1980).

Szatmary, David P., *Shays' Rebellion,* University of Massachusetts Press, 1984).

Trefousse, Hans L., *Impeachment of a President,* (University of Tennessee Press, 1975).

Wood, Gordon, editor, *The Confederation and the Constitution,* (University Press of America, 1979).

Wormuth, Francis D. and Firmage, Edwin B., *To Chain the Dog of War, The War Power of Congress in History and Law,* (SMU Press, 1986).